Taslīm: We Are the Prophets

Taslīm: We Are the Prophets

Poems on a Coptic Girlhood

CAROLYN RAMZY

MAWENZI
HOUSE

We acknowledge the support of the Canada Council for the Arts for our publishing program. We also acknowledge support from the Government of Ontario through the Ontario Arts Council, and the support of the Government of Canada through the Canada Book Fund.

Canada Council for the Arts Conseil des arts du Canada

Cover design by Sabrina Pignataro

Library and Archives Canada Cataloguing in Publication

Title: Taslīm : we are the prophets : poems on a Coptic girlhood / Carolyn Ramzy.

Names: Ramzy, Carolyn M., author.

Identifiers: Canadiana (print) 20250178451 | Canadiana (ebook) 20250181657 | ISBN 9781774151860 (softcover) | ISBN 9781774151884 (PDF) | ISBN 9781774151877 (EPUB)

Subjects: LCGFT: Poetry.

Classification: LCC PS8635.A473 T37 2025 | DDC C811/.6—dc23

Printed and bound in Canada by Coach House Printing

Mawenzi House Publishers
192 Spadina Ave, Suite 417
Toronto, ON, M5T 2C2
Canada

www.mawenzihouse.com

For my grandmothers.
For my mothers.
For M, my always.
For my two little Ns.

This is also for my village
for the عزوة *you so generously*
give me. You have made my world
a kinder place and filled it with
so much joy.

These words are for you
and for the next village
we will build.

Contents

Introduction

This book will not resonate with everyone. I fear that many Orthodox Coptic Christians might feel uncomfortable reading about the experiences and observations I share here as an Orthodox Copt growing up in diaspora.

As a feminist scholar and ethnomusicologist of Coptic music culture, I have often been accused of holding a grudge against the Coptic Church, or being a self-hating Copt for my analyses of the gendered dynamics of our expressive culture. At times, when largely male and devout readers (ie the "Orthobros," some priests bishops, and male elders) have disagreed with my scholarship and my writing, they have attempted to strip me entirely of my indigenous Coptic roots, heritage, and girlhood as punishment for airing critical thoughts about our shared world. Yet I have inherited a faith and culture that has taught me this: our repair on this earth is a labour that is intimately interconnected; only when we work together, as we do regularly in the sung liturgies that are the bedrock of our spiritual world, can we be in full communion with the best parts of ourselves and with the best parts of each other.

There are two other difficult truths I want to share: It is precisely in my most ferocious reckoning that my Coptic identity and heritage are made *mine*. It is exactly when we ask questions, air our skepticism, and reckon with our place in the world that we are truly Copts. Despite systemic and sectarian erasures, the disappearing of our indigenous Coptic tongue, the mandatory heavy chains of the Fatimid era that earned our ancestors the derogatory nickname "blue bones," our ancestors fought to survive. They struggled to keep their language, their ways of life, and their ancestral memories in their songs that they passed down to us through their own *taslīm*. It is their memories that we sing, we reckon on, and pass down this *taslīm* in our own memories.

In the Coptic diaspora, our *taslīm* does not fade even as our own memory of red dates, palm trees, and the seasonal ebbs and flows of the Nile fade and we take on other rivers, other fruits, other seas. It is our turn, even as our colloquial Egyptian Arabic yields to other languages and we sing in a new tongue. Even as unchurched Orthodox Copts in diaspora, the songs that we sing, the *kaḥk* we bake, the *mulukhiya* we have learned to make, gasping as we mix the *tasha* of *samna* with broth and mallow leaf, are all *ours*.

Here is the second difficult truth: I do hold a grudge that will resonate with some of my Coptic readers; this grudge has to do with spiritual abuse, classism, racism, sexual trauma, and systemic misogyny, which I openly discuss in this book. I often wrote poems as prayerful solace when I heard sermons from the Church pulpit regularly inviting me, as a Coptic woman, to offer my body sacrificed and broken for the sake of my community. There was never a single invitation to ever imagine myself, my body, my future, and even my afterlife solely as my own.

I want to thank those who have so bravely shared their journeys to wholeness with me, and those who have bravely shared their vulnerabilities with me so that we may grow together. I also want to thank those new to this part of my Coptic story, and who gently held me as I wrote and rewrote the final passages of this book.

It is only through your generosity—by laughing, cooking, singing, writing, reading, and labouring with me—that I can have the strength to find joy, a lived Coptic joy in the here and now. Together we can imagine Coptic villages where we can be ourselves, be a little more whole. It is also in your midst that I can imagine and embody a world with my two Coptic children in it, in their sweetest, screamiest wholeness.

You know who you are.

Your stories thread through each of these words.

And these words are for you.

I.

Taslīm

Poetry as an Autoethnography of Coptic Girlhood.

As an Egyptian Coptic Orthodox kid in the diaspora, I was always haunted by the word *taslīm*. It came as part of my deeply devotional and religious upbringing and often closely involved a set of cautionary commands:

> *"If you don't sing these alḥan, how will you pass them on to your children?"*
>
> *"If you don't learn how to make kaḥk, how will you make them for your children?"*
>
> *"If you don't go to Church, how will you take your children?"*

Used in Orthodox religious settings to acknowledge the oral transmission of heritage and ancestral knowledge from generation to generation, *taslīm* became especially heightened in my immigrant upbringing when my family moved from Egypt to Canada and then the US in the 1990s. Copts are the largest Christian religious minority in a Muslim-majority Egypt. *Taslīm* often worked on the premise of two things: that being an Orthodox Copt was deeply integrated with a devout Church experience and, for a Coptic girl, with the anticipated reproductive labours of my Coptic womanhood. Pope Shenouda III (1923-2012), one of the most influential and charismatic figures in the community, often emphasized the responsibility of mothers to raise their children in the knowledge of their Orthodox faith and identity, while concomitantly reminding women to subordinate their voices, their desires, and their bodies for the *survival* of the community. In an ascetically framed purity-focused culture, we did not have the pleasure of *wanting*. We were too busy trying to survive.

Taslīm for Coptic women, I quickly learned as a Coptic girl, was a bind of sorts. My life depended on it. *Our* lives depended on it as a community, not just in this lifetime, but also in the eternal afterlife to come, to which we truly belonged. With this promise of a deferred belonging in death, I complied, along with almost everyone I knew: I learned to sing the long and intricate liturgical hymns, the *alḥan*, as my lifeline to this heavenly place where my community would sing for eternity in *tasbīḥ*, or praise to God; and, I learned this music, knowing I would only get to sing it in a congregation, my sung labour for a heavenly belonging made intentionally inaudible for the comfort of men's piety and salvation. Over countless hours I learned to bake *kaḥk* and *petit fours* for Orthodox feast days, labouring before sink and stove alongside my grandmother and aunts, making batches large enough to feed our church community. And I sat through long and arduous services, occasionally singing myself hoarse so I could audibly and momentarily bring heaven down to earth, for myself and my kin.

As a religious minority in a Muslim-majority nation, Copts know the stakes of *taslīm* in this lived place on earth. We carry the traumatic memory of passing this knowledge in spaces that have often silenced, elided, or even violently suppressed them. Despite systemic external attempts to mute or eradicate Coptic *taslīm*, Copts have proudly and tenaciously carried on to preserve what they inherited. And while the diaspora offered a safer space for *taslīm*, Coptic immigrants faced another daunting challenge: assimilation into a new majority culture that offered other and joyous ways of being and living. I came to learn that it was often the joy of living outside of my community that seemed more threatening. In the weekly—and for some, daily—liturgical prayers across North America, the loudest congregational response during the extended service is a poignant plea to protect *taslīm* in their hyphenated progeny. As though from a slumber, folks sitting in the pews often stand and raise their hands during this sung passage, mirroring the wall at the front of the Church, displaying the icons of the saints and martyrs who had voluntarily, even joyously, given up their lives—even their own children—for this knowledge. Often, congregants tuck their babies in close against their hips as they sing. My own mother always reached for my hand, and I would trace her heavy wedding ring between my small fingers, knowing full well my precarious place in this long chain of transmission:

> *As it was and shall be, it is from*
> *generation to generation, and unto*
> *all the ages of ages. Amen.*
>
> *—the people's response, Commemoration of the saints, the Coptic Orthodox Liturgy*

Singing together was one of my most poignantly joyous yet difficult and mournful experiences. We sang to survive. And we all knew that survival comes at a cost; *Coptic taslīm* critically hinges on notions of suffering, death, embodied trauma, and self-denial of "worldly" pleasures, including food, dance, sex, and for some of the most ascetic and devout, even sleep. In her work, Coptic feminist Mariam Youssef writes about "theologies of suffering"—theological paradigms of religious communities that experience discrimination, persecution, even genocide (2020). In these spaces, generational traumas are beyond a singular event; they are the very foundation of a Coptic communal identity that routinely absorbs hurt, violence, and suffering into its definitions of who we are *there,* in Egypt, and who we are *here,* in diaspora.

Copts pride themselves on a long lineage of the martyred deaths of their saintly ancestors; in every liturgy, the graphic deaths of these saints are read aloud from a small book known as the *Synaxarium* and the dates of these deaths dictate the feast calendar of the year. The Coptic new year itself begins on one of the bloodiest days for Copts, when a mass execution of Christians accompanied the inauguration of Diocletian as Roman Emperor on September 11, 284 AD. As part of my own *taslīm,* I learned that the blood of Christians flowed through Egyptian villages like the Nile, reaching up to the knobby knees of the emperor's horses. And I learned to be proud of this viscous flow, synonymous with my pride in Egypt's flowing Nile. Once you drink from these waters, our ancestors told us, you will always return. You will always find home. In that spirit, my weepy mother marched me back from the front door, bleary-eyed and tired for my first red-eye flight to grad school and made me drink directly from the faucet of our home in a silent command: *come back home to us.*

What does it mean to grow up with religious and generational traumas as the cornerstone of our Coptic identity? What does it mean to gingerly hold the painful edges of *taslīm* with its tender joyous bends, as we pass it on from one generation to the next? And what does it mean to be part of a diaspora generation that did not experience religious discrimination firsthand, but continues to re-live it in our bodies and in our worlds, an ocean apart from our homeland, as we navigate new forms of racialized, gendered, and class-based otherings? For us diaspora Copts who do not risk life and limb to practice our faith, these conditions of belonging continue as we embody our ancestral martyrdom in other ways: deep asceticism in our daily lives, visible piety and self-denial, submission by women, public community leadership for men, community service and obligations to elders, deference to whiteness and white converts, and a strict obedience to the church hierarchy. This is how we know to live and to feel our ancestral suffering in our bones. No bloodshed needed.

As I ascend into middle adulthood, stewarding another generation of Copts as I mother my own boys, I cannot help but ask: What would it mean to define a model of *taslīm* to *repair* and *reckon* with our intergenerational traumas, and not *relive* them over and over again? As I shift into Coptic elderhood, I wonder: What if we tried to imagine ourselves without our suffering and instead with joy, maybe even a little pleasure? And as my afro greys, I try to imagine: Who in ourselves would we meet on the other side of our suffering? What version of our ancestors would we become . . . and one day, maybe even pass on?

As we rewrite these maps of being into life, we break new pathways that often lead us to the unknown, and many times we have to forge ahead without our kin. We simply don't have the privilege of our elders to guide us, having been pushed out of our communities into a sort of cultural, social, and spiritual exile when we attempted to imagine something different. Some people call this experience a form of *un/churching*. Yet even as we leave the Church, the Church never quite leaves us, having imprinted itself onto our bodies and minds long after we leave. It is a bind of another kind: to look into the deep horizon of new possibilities for life while yearning with nostalgia for an uneasy familiar: eating our mother's home cooking without our full selves at the table, standing in the pews singing our favourite hymns, praying with words that leave little cuts and bruises over our bodies, spirit, and imagination. At new tables, we still pine for the familiar smells and sounds of the hands that baked us into being and the songs that formed our hearts. As I ascended into motherhood, I could not bear to watch my children's wings clipped so that they too could belong and grow in the community. In the grief of my loss for the familiar and my twinned fear and hope for something different, I forged a nest in between and betwixt my worlds, repairing my own wings by their side as I taught them to use theirs. I thought it would be lonely out here, but I was wrong. There are so many fellow sojourners in this place. We are reckoning and repairing while rearing a new generation of un/Orthodox(ing) Copts.

Audre Lorde's words in her influential 1978 essay, "Uses of the Erotic," come to mind: "recognizing the power of the erotic within our lives can give us the energy to pursue genuine change within our worlds . . . " She defines the erotic from the Greek *eros*, the personification of love in all of its aspects, born of Chaos, and personifying creative power and harmony—and importantly, being a critical life force in women. The erotic, she argues, is a dynamic and lived reclaiming of this creative energy, the knowledge of which we as women can reclaim in our language, our history, our dancing, our loving, our work, our lives—and even our faith to become gods, saints, and villains in our own life stories.

What would Coptic womanhood look like with this power fully celebrated, bodies not sequestered in shame but honoured for their miraculous transitions, voices not quieted but amplified, curls not straightened and covered but out like a lion's mane? What would it be like to embrace the pleasure we feel in our bodies not as a curse but a medium to repair our ancestral wounds? I lean on Lorde's words, and that of other Black and racialized queer activists and scholars, to imagine and enact a world in which *taslīm* is not a burden of suffering but rather a lived labour of joy and liberation. I imagine that it is this shared work towards a collective liberation that will interlink us with our past while we rewrite our futures, and potentially, rewrite these futures with new kin, new allies, and new villages. In other words, I lean on Lorde's words to fulfill the promise of my Orthodox ancestors: to live working for the promise of a better tomorrow brings heaven down under my dancing feet.

As it was and shall be, it is from
generation to generation, and unto
all the ages of ages. Amen.

I share these poems, which I started writing while sitting in my Church's pews, as an autoethnography of my Coptic girlhood. And I write it to index larger questions of Coptic girlhood, holy song, and a desire for a whole sexuality and *taslīm* that have not only shaped my own life, but the lives of many Coptic women. I turn to Susan Faulkner's insistence that poetry is political practice, for the ways it allows us to openly talk about hard things, and for the ways it mirrors the use of veiled metaphors so prevalent in our Egyptian colloquial speech, and in our Coptic hymns and spiritual songs. Faulkner reminds us that this hidden interplay is political for the ways in which it bypasses stifling social structures and allows marginalized groups (within marginalized groups) to represent themselves. Poetry, she insists, is a feminist practice, treading a blurred line as social research, autoethnography, and even a kind of visionary activism making way for a kind of world-making (2017). In many ways, I write to hold onto the promise of a Coptic afterlife in my own hands too: when we sing, heaven's lived promised echoes back. That is why we sing until we get there, until we die, and until we can finally sing a sound for an eternity—"praising continuously without ceasing" (from the Prayer of Reconciliation, St Basil's Coptic Orthodox Liturgy).

Yet I also write to live. I write to live as an academic. And, I write as a Coptic woman, leaning into poetry's transgressive dimensions to demand repair and change in my overlapping worlds. I write to say what we could not sing as Copts, as immigrants, and as Coptic immigrant women. Importantly, I lean on Renato Rosaldo's notion of *antropoesía,* poetry informed by his own 2014 ethnography of grief to showcase the triple bind of diaspora Coptic girlhood; Coptic women are not only stranded in the liminal third spaces of diaspora experience, assimilating to a new homeland, language, and culture, but we are often left out of the Coptic community's rhetoric of belonging in what anthropologist Joseph Youssef and others have noted is an increasingly asceticizing Orthodox culture in the Coptic diaspora (2019). In other words, Coptic women are often dialectically positioned between life and a kind of spiritual death, as critical to men's salvation while problematizing our very presence based on our gender and sex. Never mind the thick soup of white supremacy, structural racism, and neoliberal capitalism that we navigate in our new settler homelands, our thick curls brandished both as shields but also serving as the occasional target.

In this book, I imagine and create a world in which a Coptic *taslīm* is kinder, maybe even a little reparative. I draw on poetry's anticolonial possibilities to tell my story as part of a longer arc that takes me back to my grandmothers, their grandmothers, and the grandmothers before them in lives that saw Arab conquests, British colonialism, and religious patriarchy that curtailed women's wants, voices, and desires.

It was only two generations ago that my paternal grandmother was married off at sixteen and produced both her sons by the age of eighteen. It was her generation that went to American missionary schools in Upper Egypt, inheriting the well-known *'odit al-khawaga* or "the foreigner's complex"—a leftover colonial legacy that shaped our community's desire for lighter skins, straight hair, skinnier bodies, and lighter-coloured eyes—and passed it down to us in their own *taslīm*. It is often against these Eurocentric standards that our mothers taught us to see ourselves, holding up our dark eyes, dark curly hair, and curvaceous bends to the mirror like a sacrifice to white supremacy—*Here, we can fix that*. When our summer sun-kissed skin came in, we learned to apologize for the unfettered outside joy that darkened our limbs. When sweat converted our straightened hair back to curly, we laboured long and hard to minimizes the effects.

Yet, it is also in the ruptures in their stories that our grandmothers sang, binding their wounds with faith, hope, and song to find their joy, to bake sun bread, to mend dresses for *eid*, and to gasp over the wafts of *mulukhiya* or mallow soup on the stove. They taught us to sing when things got hard.

Many of the poems and stories I share here are drawn from my diary entries, napkin poetry, Whatsapp messages, and hushed conversations that I heard between hymns (*alḥan*), sermons, and other Arabic spiritual songs (*taratīl*), trying to make sense and imagine a life outside the Church. I wrestle with the questions that my younger self quietly asked, tucked against my mother's hip as we both sang *from generation to generation*. The writing often helped me to pass the time, and more importantly, helped me to process the gentle sadness I shared with my family, my kin, and my village, yearning to belong to a heavenly nation in our deaths, ready to die as martyrs tomorrow, but not yet ready to live for today.

But I so badly want to live.

And I have quietly learned that many of us want to do that too.

We Are the Prophets

We are the prophets our mothers were looking for
  their yearnings unrequited.
We are the dreams
  they saw in their reflections,
and when they looked down into our faces.

We are the pinch of blood swilling in the mouth
when they held their piece for peace.
We are the crooks of the elbows
bearing
the weight of unrequited children to an unrequiting world.
We are the unfolding of the curls, beating back the heat of a colonial singe
into unruly silver, then grey, then a gentle henna copper against the sun.

We are the lifeline running from palm to palm, the quiet thread of *taslīm* from hand to hand

arriving

on the back of many little deaths, and new life slipping into this world.

We are all these quiet moments distilled into a lifetime of restlessness.

Requiting.

Relentless while relenting.

We are
giving into the Giving.
Then taking the Taking.
Falling headfirst into the Dreaming.

+++

Coptic Villainy

when the Arabic tongue swallowed us whole
starting the seventh century

we made sure to pepper it with
enough Coptic

that you can hear us in it every day

and everywhere.

Can you imagine what we will do with the English?

II.

On Coptic Mothers and Mothering

Tayta.

I remember, once Mama, Tayta, and I stood together to bake. Having stolen my cherry bathrobe, Tayta stood there, the smaller and shorter of us three. And there we were, three generations, each with our separate stories and the divide of three countries between us. Our hands sunk in batter. Tayta's hands glittered and I marveled at the story each grooved line sang. I imagine her voice saying, "One for your aunt Isis, one for Shadia, one for your mother Mango, and a myriad of lines for their babies, each by name. For the banana bread I've baked for you, for the mouth that kissed you on the cheek, for your Gedo [grandfather]*. And for each line, a song, a* tartīla *to teach you to sing with me, so your hands will always sing with the simplest of tasks."*

February 1, 2007
Personal Diary

⁜⁜⁜

I was in my late teens when my grandmother, Ogeni, decided that my thick and short frame was perfect for baking. Among my taller cousins, I was closest to the sink to do the dishes and looked like I had the right vigor to pound dough into bread and shape batter into cookies. Every year from my midteens to my early twenties, she dragged me to her long baking sessions where we would make special cookies for *eid*—the Coptic Orthodox feasts like Christmas and Easter. Known as *kaḥk* and *petits fours,* these cookies bore the markings of Ottoman and French occupations, inherited and rewritten by all Egyptians not as symbols of subjection but of feasting. These cookies were hard to make but were the hallmark of all religious festivities in Egypt, for Muslims and Christians alike.

Despite the wide array of cookie presses available, Tayta did everything by hand. We painstakingly shaped each petal of the intricate flowers, baked them, and then coated each flower with jam to stick them together to make small delicate sandwiches. Drawing on a Mamluk Egyptian inheritance, we stuffed *kaḥk* with walnuts or nougats to replace the golden coins that the pious traditionally handed out as alms during and after major religious feasts. But first we had to roll them into buttery balls. They too had to be individually shaped. Side by side, we sat together for hours as we gently pressed the smiling face of each cookie with a pastry crimper, deep enough to hold a dusting of powdered sugar, but not so much that it gave away the cookie's hidden treasures. These shifts for making cookies were long and arduous, from as early as six in the morning and into the night for two to three days at a time. Tayta only stopped for two breaks: one for lunch and another for tea. And because it was lent (*siam*), when we Copts abstained from meat or dairy products, we could not taste these ghee- and butter-laden sweets until the *eid* a few weeks later.

Yet, regardless of the hard labour for her aging and shrinking frame, my grandmother insisted on making two batches of cookies, *kaḥk* and *petits fours*, for almost every Coptic family in Rochester, New York—there were about 60 families at the time—where she lived with my aunt, until she died in 2007.

It was these baking sessions that introduced me to the constitutive power of *taratīl* (s. *tartīla*), the most popular nonliturgical, colloquial Arabic songs in the Coptic Orthodox community. Their origins go back to translated American and British missionary songs, and they form the most ubiquitous popular religious genre in the Middle East, especially among Egypt's Christian denominations. They draw on vernacular Arabic, widely known Egyptian folk motifs, and popular Egyptian (and imported) melodies. As little ditties, *taratīl* and *taranīm* range from quiet and intoned prayers, a cappella folk songs that frame and punctuate community gatherings, to the loud rock-concert hits, satellite music videos, and even cellphone ringtones that fill Egypt's Muslim soundscapes, as subtle public declarations of Christian presence. In other words, *taratīl* permeate Egyptian Christian soundscapes in one way or another, virtually and viscerally, both in Egypt and abroad. My grandmother and I would sing these songs in the late 1990s and early 2000s, like millions of Christians in Egypt and the Coptic diaspora, in Arabic as well as the languages of their new homes. These songs, alongside the more liturgical *alḥan*, frame Coptic spaces, Coptic selves, and the stories that many Copts tell about their place in this world and in their afterlife to come."

While Tayta and I waited for bread to rise and for cookies to brown, she almost always pulled out a small hymn book, *Kitab al-Taranīm* (Book of Taranīm), and nestled it between our ghee-glazed arms so we could sing to pass the time and to ease our labour. Given that I had immigrated to North America as a child, she would gently fit the forgotten Arabic back into my mouth and wait patiently as I *fuk al-khat*, untangle the Arabic consonants to sound out the words. She would nudge me along as I drew on the remnants of my second-grade education in Kuwait to recognize and read the texts. When I finally managed it, she would teach me the melody and we would sing and chat for hours, hiding the pride that I learned to fish for in her half smile.

It was between these traditional *taratīl* and *taranīm* sessions that my grandmother would tell me about her life before her marriage, motherhood, and immigrating to the US. I relished her quiet stories and their details. Tayta never spoke much until she sang. When I was still an undergraduate, she shared with me a pivotal moment in her life: the day she traded her university education for a piano, all so that she could play her favourite *taratīl* by ear. I remember leaning in to listen to her intently, the irony of my attendance at a prestigious music conservatory not lost on us both.

Tayta Ogeni was born in 1923, the same year that Egypt's pioneering feminist, Huda Sha'rawi founded the Egyptian Feminist Union (see Badran 1995). She was the daughter of a prominent cotton exporter, Atalla Faltas, and she and her family split their time between her Upper Egyptian birth village in Girga and coastal Alexandria, where her father exported cotton to Britain. As a girl from Upper Egypt she was lucky to have a high school education. Close to graduation her principal took her aside and gently advised her to continue on to university, a rare but prestigious compliment in her time. But when she approached her father with this idea, he flatly refused. It was painful enough, he told her, to part with her brothers when they went to boarding school in Alexandria. He simply could not do without her or her sisters, and they had to stay at home. Tayta remembered that she cried for days, pleading, but her father would not budge. After the last and most extended quarrel, he approached her with a proposal: If he were to buy her a piano, would she make peace and stay home? Tayta agreed. Stunned, I heard that she acquiesced to giving up her dream of a university education for a piano. Instead of studying at university, she filled the house with the sounds of *taratīl* and *taranīm,* which she played by ear. She did not learn enough of the Western musical notation to be able to play anything else.

I always recall Tayta's story with a particular sadness. That conversation explained so much about her, and the hidden subtexts of our many conversations. Whenever she read my fortune in the bottom of a *fingan* (cup), her fingers dusted with cardamom coffee, she frequently made me promise to finish my own education before getting married. While singing our favourite *taratīl*, she would ask me about my schooling and forecast my travels to conferences by the ceramic pathways revealed by the coffee grinds: *your papers,* she'd tell me as I leaned in earnestly, *are as white as snow and your presentation will go well. But see that dark spot there? Someone in your audience will ask you a hard question* (and they did!).

Unable to attend university, she busied herself preparing for another kind of schooling for Egyptian girls: motherhood. Thanks to her upper-class habitus, she attended sewing classes, learned how to cook and bake, and regularly attended Orthodox Coptic services at her local church until she got married on September 17, 1947, in her mid-twenties, to a young lawyer. She raised three daughters who all went on to university. One daughter became one of the first women to study medicine in her class, another studied pharmacy, and my own mother pursued a degree in English literature. Along the way, Tayta ensured that they all learned how to sing *taratīl* and play them on her piano. That piano and these songs followed her from home to home, from Girgia to Sohag, and to her apartment in Cairo's prestigious Abbassiyya district where her husband practiced law. And having immigrated to the United States in 1985, she made one of my aunts buy her a new piano in Rochester, New York. Over the rich aroma of coffee and tea, as we crimped cookies and shaped bread, Tayta continued to fill my aunt's house with song.

When she passed away in 2007, at the funeral service I stood in front of Rochester's Coptic Orthodox Church to bid her farewell and sang her favourite *tartīla*. As the deadening realization hit me that this was the last time I would sing *taratīl* with her, I marveled: Tayta was everywhere in this place yet nowhere at the same time. As part of the Church congregation, we had all feasted on her cookies and tasted her bread.

When we looked forward in the direction of the altar, the most sacred space that separated the all-male team of priests, readers, and deacons from the mixed congregation, her presence still framed the doorway in the curtains she had delicately sewed with her hands. In the front pews where an exclusively male choir stood to direct her favourite *taratīl,* deacons still wore the red and gold sashes, *badrashayn,* whose frayed ends she had mended. In a gentle irony, her favourite *tarnīma* was a soothing lullaby about the impossibility of a mother forgetting her child, only to be rescued by the Lord. Even in her passing, Tayta seemed to forget no one. As I sang, struggling to maintain my voice, congregants walked forward to pass her casket. The spot in the second pew where she always stood was empty. People wept.

In 'Unsa Min 'Um al-Hanun (If a Compassionate Mother Forgets):

If a compassionate mother forgets me, my Lord will hold me closely
For him, children are more cherished, so how can he forget me?
How can he forget me? If a mother forgets her newborn child,
*My Lord will not forget me.**

+++

* You can hear this tartīla here: @CopticWomenSingToo, https://www.instagram.com/p/CRPnftOgh0H/.

kaḥk.

It is mesmerizing.
To watch new small hands sink into the batter. *my sons.*
My mind's eye shifts to a double vision: Tayta's hands glistening with *samna,* ghee,
the lines on her palms leaving an imprint in the dough.
All I have to do is follow.

ḥissīha, she would say. *feel it, then you will know.*

She too follows the lines printed before her.
And I wonder what her mind's eye sees in its double vision:
Rooftop ovens. Her mother. Circles and circles of women chatting and working and singing.
Small hands covered with flour, glowing with ghee. Hands that raised three babies and mourned the death of one. The fourth golden bracelet she wears is for her only son. Lifelines weaving a continuous thread, crowning at the wrist.

My boys have such small hands. Upside smiles reflect back at us in the bowl. The frantic scramble to be the first and to be the last.
With each handful of batter, I am now the one leaving trails to follow.

ḥissuha, habaybi. I whisper to them. *Feel it and then you will know, my loves.*

matriarchy and memory work in tandem,
waḥid bisalim liltanī.
One passes it on to the next
cookie after cookie.
kaḥkaya warra kaḥkaya.

This is where our histories are written. Sometimes sung.
Sometimes not.
Walnuts stuffed in the warm embrace of the yeasty dough.
A *na'sha* drawn to hold a dusting of sugar.

the afterlife of sun bread.

for Tayta

I write
to meet you
in this poem,
imagine you back at my table
offering me
sun bread
as witness to the new feasts
I have learned to make
and the new *aghaby*
I have learned to
host in my own kitchen.

I imagine the gentle pinch
of your mouth
when I tell you
that I finished university,
that I am the professor now

I write
to see
the way your eyes gleam
when I point out
my two boys
their rambunctious hands
already roaming the table
pulling on the hem and edge of
dress and *mafrash* in a
cacophony of
mama mama mama

and we'll lock eyes and
smile over their curly heads

as I lean forward
and part the loaf
you and I have always shared

to give them a slice.

Mama.

A child, I dutifully stood next to my mother in our little church every Sunday, in our small and segregated suburban town in Upstate New York. We had a routine: as soon as we found our pew, we filed quietly in, and after I had passed her the lace head scarf (*escharpe*) to cover our hair, we sang loud, smiling and covered through the four to five hours of service. We stood together at the front of the pews, behind my aunt and grandmother, and our loud voices often attracted stares from the deacons leading the service at the front of the church. We pretended we could not see them. Sometimes I would trace the length of her long knobby fingers, feel the roundness of her wedding ring, and sneak it off to try it on, to weigh its heaviness. And when her voice faltered in the liturgy and she began to weep, I would cry with her and lend her strength in my own tears.

Weeping was part of the ascetic comportment of Orthodox piety and prayer. Often stories of ascetic monks and saints—*good* Copts—include passages about tears of repentance and contrition, tears of purification, and finally, tears of release from our heavy human existence. Beside the stories of these virginal and faithful victors, I know she also wept over the burdens of a lopsided marriage, traumas of immigration, and a significant drop in her class status after she left Kuwait. She came from an affluent family and had married below her class. Immigration to North America pulled her down even further, and the memories of a richer more comfortable life in the Gulf were just that, bittersweet memories. In a biting irony, she now worked as a secretary in her brother-in-law's family practice, all while my own father and I cleaned the same office as janitors. Our standing order in church, one pew behind my aunt and my father and brothers, one pew behind my uncle, was a replica of this silent and well understood social order. And when we dispersed out of the pews into the *Aghaby* coffee hour in the church basement, my aunt, uncle, maternal cousins and other affluent congregants would often remind us of this class order, just in case we had forgotten it in the jolly looseness of buttered bagels and black tea in Styrofoam cups.

My mother did her best to inform me about this order, the place she had inherited. She was the youngest of three sisters, having arrived on the heels of the prized baby boy in her family, who however had died. She was also the darkest of her sisters. She often reminded me of this and joked about how her sisters had attempted to wash her skin to make it white. All they managed was an irritating tanned pink. She often laughed when she told this story, and I would uncomfortably bury my eyes into my wheat-coloured forearms. She also had the kinkiest hair, which I had inherited and which regularly bristled against the discipline of the curling iron. Her sisters, my *tantes,* and my grandmother, all helped her endure the singe of the *maqwa,* the iron, to coif it straight. Every day except for when she was working abroad, where she wore it large and natural in an afro. Then she got married and it went back to straight. Then she developed breast cancer and was excused the ordeal.

Strange, the forgiveness from the *maqwa* that only comes with migration. Or sickness. Or having no hair at all.

My mother first straightened my hair when I was six, and then chemically relaxed it when I was 10. I remember the day clearly, a milestone between the worlds of kinky brillo curls to shiny straightness. It was then one of the happiest days of my life, when I tightly gripped the box of Dark & Lovely in my hands and imagined my hair as straight as shown on the cover. Until the curls came back. They always came back. But my mother and I persisted. We straightened this beast chemically every few months, until one day, at the tender and delicate age of 35, pregnant and barfing from the stench, I finally stopped. As the baby in my belly grew, as I imagined his own little tufts of hair, I began to meet the underbelly of my own curls for the first time. I was struck by their newness and curl. And I was humbled by their resilience, even their generosity to come back to me after so many years of blatant abuse and denial. *Hello old friends, it's nice to see you.*

When we immigrated and lived close to my aunts, I fell in line behind my cousins and knew my order in our world: I was the poor, short, dark, curvy and curly to their wealthy, tall, fair, thin and straight. When they outgrew their designer clothing, they let me have them. This was the ancestral knowledge that my mother had accepted. This was her place in the world. And like a good Copt, she desperately worked to pass it on. I remember the evenings of those exchanges, the feeling of both glee and terror that some clothing *might* fit. Both my aunt and my mother would take deep breaths and lean back into their chairs when many of the clothes did not fit: *ya khusra* . . . that's too bad, the aunts would sigh together like synchronized swimmers, eyeing my thick middle with disdain. And I would lean back too, trying desperately to breathe in, learning for the first time the cutting power of words. But I would beg to keep trying, smiling to persist, to fit my roundness into all the tightnesses. And I would feel honoured to be compared to the oldest, prettiest, and light-skinned cousin who had dieted and shed a lot of weight in her teens. At the time she wore green contact lenses, straightened her hair and dyed it blond. I could be *an almost* to her original almost. One high school year, I was so desperate, I stopped eating for a few weeks. I learned how to make myself throw up with a delicious religious hotness. I persisted until I got sick. In the quiet and solitary recovery afterwards, as I curled up alone and sweaty on the living room couch, I carved out my first secret under Mama's unsuspecting gaze:

I love myself too much for this.

And I love the joy of food too much too, more than I love the designer clothes.

A Forgotten Entry in the Synaxarium for Our Wounded Matriarchs

Our mothers and our sisters who have fallen asleep, whose souls the Church has taken, repose them.

Our matriarchs
nursed our earliest wounds,
becoming our
first judges
to help us
survive a world
bent on our exile
to the small
and quiet.

Standing on their shoulders
we remember them
each by name,
how they struggled,
pressing us forward
with their urgent
palms on our backs.

Let us read and recite the names of our holy mothers,
sisters, daughters, grandmothers, and tantes
all those who have fallen asleep and
whom the Church has taken from us,
that we may repose their souls,
and that we too may accord them our mercy
and forgive.

because,
they too were slowly ground down
song to song
sermon to sermon
Sunday to Sunday
and driven
far from us

Sali | Pray
they tell us

So, we pray in
their holy names that we may
rise a little higher,
to stand just a hair
taller
on their clipped shoulders,

with our hips
round
and abundant,
and our hair
big and out,

taking up space

for all of us.

Amen.

to mama

i have sat
at length
with your reprimands,
about my lack of
endurance
and chided myself,
not for the pain to be smaller
but for my own stamina
to grow
and embrace this pain as a gift
as our martyrs once did.

then i too
became a mother
and learned
how to expand and bend,
to cradle and kiss
each scratch
on each scrapped knee

to embrace their skin
like a protecting callus,
to bring them into me
with their fullness

and it is in this
you have gifted me
the most.

Coptic FGM

had it not been for a mother
back along our ancestral line,
we too would have been circumcised,

our
clitoris
clipped
and
creased

for an imaginary
virtue

that did not account
for
the monthly bleed.

who's the martyr now?

Synaxarium Disrupted: to my sons.

when you arrived,
I arrived
to mother you

and to mother me too

I vow
not to offer you as martyrs
to this world
but to cradle you in

to undo, curl by curl,
some of the harm I inherited
so that you will stand
just a hair
taller on my
shoulders.

and as my fingers
caressed the very
first twitchings
of your smiling mouths
you taught me
to imagine
a world
with my own mouth
smiling
wide and open

i won
my own spirit
when I refused
to hand you
over blind
and folded
to the dictates of
religious law

learning through the grit of this bitter
and sweet labour
that
it is *you*
who give birth to
me.

III.

the priests, the bishops, and the converts

On Faith: for a priest of an oriental church.

Do you believe in God?

Once I stood in one of those English-language-only Coptic churches when a priest would not talk to me unless I told him that I believed in God; apparently my reputation as an academic had transformed me into an atheist. This question, he told me, was the prerequisite to chat. Under the neon lights of the church basement, I could not help but wonder why the price of conversation with him was higher for me than for the White convert he so readily approached in his own services. I wondered why my own survival, written in the curve of each curl, was not enough. Nor was the wheat colour of my face, mirroring the smiling silhouettes of the martyrs in the gold leaf backdrop of Coptic icons in his Church *iconostasis*. Like the saints in these written portals to God, I too held the promise of a shared *theosis*, a oneness with the divine, a oneness with fellow Copts, and maybe even a oneness with him, the priest.

But he insisted:

Do you believe in God?

I refused to answer. Recalling other spiritual evictions from this holy place, the priest cornered me. Against his coercion for a public confession, I finally replied: "My faith is between me and God."

"So you *do* believe!"

His reply sounding incredulous, as though he did not *believe* me. Because the only way he assumed I could believe was to remain churched and secure under his surveillant eye, to take communion from his hands into my mouth, to do so in the right order, to fast, to carry a comportment that bent my body in submission to his, to kiss his hands. Here's what I wished I could tell him: in refusing this hierarchy, I could finally imagine a more divine way to encounter the Divine. I could not share my grief with him about a faith made so small and fragile that a little difference between us could dismantle his entire Coptic world.

As coerced confessions go, he only received the partial truth. There was simply no safe way to confess to him that I have faith in God the same way that I have faith in people. I could not confess to him that, like my mother and a long line of mothers before her, I had learned to recalibrate my faith into a stubborn and lived hope, into one of a transgressive joy while daily navigating the exclusionary politics of the clerical patriarchy, daily bouts with racism, and a continued coloniality that tainted our collective Coptic inheritance. I think of my grandmother sitting at the piano she gave up for her school education, her fingers joyously playing out the translated missionary songs meant to woo her away from her faith, only to bring her closer to it, and to burn into her the desire to send each daughter to university. She played on as she witnessed each daughter finish university, and the daughters of her daughters become writers, professors, and physicians. Instead of being defeated by my great-grandfather's patriarchy, my grandmother sang her faith into this piano's imperial ears, making it *sing back to her*. She made that piano sing while we baked *kaḥk* for *eid*, while she stitched the rich velvet vestments for the local priest to wear, while she baked Lenten banana bread without milk and eggs and fed the disappearing Arabic language into her grandchildren's mouths. In my last images of her, this piano sang as she rounded out her final loafs of sun bread (*'ayish shamsi*). Traditionally baked on Upper Egyptian rooftops, she made it rise under New York's wintery skies.

Tayta's faith and the one she passed on to me is a generous one, that everyone—churched, the unchurched, skeptic, and even those traumatized by religious coercions that did not feed their souls—all belonged around the table, and in the oneness of Christ. I have no doubt that, at her table before she fed him, dousing morsels of bread in rich *mulukhiya,* my grandmother would have never asked this priest of an oriental church:

Do you believe in God?

The Bishops.

how is it that we ask bakers who have never baked
to feed us bread.

bakers who spit on sun loaves
not as our rightful sustenance
but as a curse for making us hungry

how is it that we ask healers who have yet to heal
to doctor us to health

doctors who spit on our living bodies
not as evidence of the daily miraculous
but rather as flaws that deserve their deaths

how is it that we have designated celibate men
as gatekeepers of our sexuality
men who have yet to break bread
and watch the steam rise,
reminding us to live.

Orthobros.

Orthobros
patrol
the net
using colonial batons
as they
bleed from
the ears

their anger aching
from a loss
of place
and tongue

that they cram
fallen morsels
from the empire's
table into their mouths

and call
it a
feast.

Al-kanīsa: Sit. Stand. Repeat.

Arrival entails a quick slot into your spot.
quick and quiet so no one can hear you—
escharpe. matted lipstick. coiffed but covered. perfect—
and look straight ahead to the hollowed ostrich egg.
Contemplate that pious look of desperate belief.
Tilt your head to the right. Make that listening face.
Maybe pout. Give an occasional nod, but not too vigorous.
don't make eye contact.

Then

Sit. Stand. Repeat.
Sit. Stand. Down to your knees.

Coptic *kapt*

when did my Coptic collarbone take on the same currency as
my breast?

when did that happen to my face?
when I looked up to sing in Church or raise my voice to
petition
this *kapt.*

when did my protesting arm threaten your purity
like the raw sight of my vulva?

you wish.

did it occur to you that your beardly manifestations
parallel the same Coptic coif of your below,

but I know how to control myself.

do you?

IV.

Coptic Church As Woman

Coptic Church As Woman.

Coptic Orthodox girlhood is often unrequited.
Unless you are born lucky, or privileged,
or white and then convert.

It starts early. Coptic mothers who birth girls must wait eighty days to baptize them, delaying their induction into the Orthodox community and extending their exile from a heavenly belonging forty days longer than boys. With baptism as the key to a heavenly entry, daughters learn early to wait for this promised salvation of their souls. Apparently, even hair-less and body-less in the afterlife, there is segregated seating in heaven too.

Girls who bleed cannot take communion.

Mothers who birth have to be absolved because they survive and bleed.

And widows who stop bleeding take communion last.

Orthodox funerary ritual begs for women's continual absolution after death—for daring to live, to fuck, to birth, and even daring to die (see Youssef 2025).

As Copts, we know that the cost of life is the blood of someone else who dies, a martyr, a Christ. But it was not just Christ bleeding up on the cross. Mary birthed him, bleeding too. And sopped up his blood pooled beneath the cross with her veil, her own heart splayed open and bleeding. But we never sing about that, what it must have been like to stain your hands with the blood of your own child.

In the church in Upstate New York where I grew up, widows dressed in black for the remainder of their lives after their husbands passed. They took communion last. As they waited in line for the Eucharist, after the virgins and married women, they highlighted the quiet hierarchic and value of Coptic womanhood in our community. After a lifetime of service, their weary bodies would now sag against the walls, standing against them for ease. Girls would then run up with chairs for them to alleviate their wait. And as we did so, we were aware of the order and value of our use too.

As an academic later, I could not help but notice the dissonances of a religious institution keen on purifying our bodies while singing in our name as women. I had studied works of scholars who had noted the ways that early gendered nationalisms imagined Egypt as a woman during the struggle for sovereignty from British colonial rule (Baron 2005). I could not help but see the parallel of a Coptic Church *as* woman. The *kanīsa,* church, is gendered female in Arabic, and many religious songs (*taratīl, taranīm, tasbīḥa, and alḥan*) often used maternal imagery and idioms—saintly mothers, desert *'amas*—as metaphors to embody the strategic politics of minority belonging in Egypt. Our songs and hymns—a lifeline to our heavenly belonging—are replete with these gendered motifs, often bleeding too. Yet, in the same breadth, Orthodox clerics also use these very metaphors to discipline and quiet women's bodies, voices, and lives *within* the community. It is a strange double bind, to both be dialectically positioned as critical to community survival while reckoning with our bodies as potentially threatening to our community's salvation. I think back to the words of my youth, concomitantly recited in praise while also poised as a pointed threat.

> *If you don't sing these alḥan, how will you teach them to your children?*
>
> *If you don't learn how to make kaḥk, how will you make them for your children?*
>
> *If you don't go to Church, how will you take your children?*

As a child, I sang for the children I would have. For the mother I would be. For the widow I might become, knowing that both the order and value of my use was predicated upon whom I would produce and for whose sake.

Even our heavenly nation, *al-sama,* where we hope to return to spend eternity, is gendered female. The eucharistic bread, the *orbana,* which is transformed into the living body of the Christ is also gendered as female as it is kneaded, as it is stamped by a wooden seal that pierces the doughy flesh five times to replicate Christ's suffering. And yet when it is women who bleed—to menstruate, to birth, to give life—they are barred from this holy re/union. And when they finally stop bleeding, they wait to take communion last, their bodies sagging against the walls.

I often sat in the church pews and spent the better part of my career with this dissonance cradled in my hands, wondering why a heavenly salvation or damnation hinged on our silence and the thin skin of hymen between our legs. What is the irony that both these folds of skin sing, often in that intertwined melody of pleasure and pain? In my seat, I chewed on bitter and harsh words like *'ayb* or "shame" and *haram* between my teeth when all I wanted to do was to sing, to be heard, to disagree, maybe even dare to say *no.* I chewed on the uneasy interpolation of a woman's voice with her *pudenda* or privates, that somehow, a Coptic singing mouth could really be read as a crooning Coptic pussy.

Really?

But maybe they are right: to sound out loud is the direct desire to be heard and seen.

And I quickly learned: desire is dangerous.

Especially as a Copt. And most especially, as a Coptic woman.

✢✢✢

Coptic curls.

my coptic curls have
been a thorn in your side
since the moment they defied
your eighty-day rule.
when they
wafted up over the waves of the baptismal font
and soaked up each drop of holy *myron* oil.

Girl

and still

holy.

since then
my coptic curls keep pricking you
drawing blood
as they defy
your hairless imagination
of my bits
and your priests keep
asking me
again and again
in your holy sacrament of confession:

did you cum?

Good Coptic Girlhood

Good Coptic girlhood
only works
if you're white
or
if you're a man.

Unequal conversions

i wish i could convert into your whiteness
as easily as you can convert into my Coptic-ness
so that i too may be met
with the generous unfurling
of knowledge and space,
that I may be invited
to speak at the bishop's table
to sup on soup
of marrow and bone
in a way that my
Coptic girl self
cannot
in both
whiteness
and
in
Ortho
doxy.

parking lot converts

for f

before church
we are the
parking-lot converts
who sit
eye-to-eye
in the rear-view mirror
praying to
look closer than we appear

clenched fists on wheel
we sit

as we
strip and
corset stitch
one layer
over another
to cross the threshold

of a little
homeland church
for a little
home

don't smile too much
don't talk too much
don't disagree
don't be disabled
don't resist too much
don't be gay
don't be poor

don't be a feminist
don't be trans
don't be progressive
don't take up space
don't be fat
don't *be* too much
and don't ask questions.

Just relent,

to the narrow
Coptic life of home
that the *abuna* partitions
in his hands,
like a holy *orbana* that
only he can touch.

al-kapt II

to think

about how they kept us
from rooms within our own house
held the contents
under lock and key
held heaven
hostage
to
justify
the daily famine
pulsing
in our soft
underbellies

so that when we grow,

we must peel back the
jagged edges
scale by scale
and wonder
what the softness
was like
before we had
to harden
and
live
under the staircase
of our own
house,

fills me with rage.

an anthropology of all that is *haram.*

my body
is an anthropology
of all that is *haram.*

in the
study of
each curve and crevice

they taught me
all the bits
i could
not
touch

or savour
in my own
                mouth.

even my brain
had to become
a holy temple so that

i
could not ask
hard questions and

curiosity
became

haram.

V.

in the beginning, there was lola

I was a good Coptic Orthodox girl.

I was a good Coptic Orthodox girl. Or at least I tried. I tried hard.

I fasted. I prayed. And throughout my teens, I taught Sunday school. I often straightened my hair, taking three hours to coif this ancestral afro, only to cover it with a lace veil, an *escharpe,* during the long Coptic Orthodox services. And I endured. Tight lipped and smiley, I watch the anguished hairs succumb to the mockery of heat and humidity under the sleuthing eyes of my Egyptian *tantes*. They too sat similarly straightened and coiffed in the next pew, all of us a portrait for the colonial singe of the *maqwa,* the hot iron. But I persisted. We all persisted. I mirrored the *tantes* in many ways: I crossed my ankles below the pew and pulled the hem of my dress down to below the knee. I pressed my lips closed and clean. I learned how to tilt my head piously rightward during the priest's sermons every Sunday, sometimes biting down my lower lip or inner cheek quietly for colour and contour, as my hands traced the battered edges of clandestine romance novels, Anne Rice's *Interview with the Vampire* series, and Sylvia Plath's *Bell Jar* that I had snuck in. To pass the time during the five-hour weekly service, I relieved my boredom writing poetry on napkins and scraps of paper. I often wrote in my journal. And I timed it all just right so I could fall into the outward rhythm of prayer:

Sit. Stand. Repeat. Sit. Stand. Down to your knees.

Yet even after all the hours of pious and coiffed comportment, timed weeping, palms lifted in prayer to mirror the icons of the Orthodox saints as they cradled the heavens in their ascetic hands, even after I learned that one should abstain from sex the night before Holy Communion, I masturbated every night for most of my youth (and funnily enough, I still do). During Orthodox liturgy, I noted with twinges of angst and guilty victory my two parallel lives, my Coptic life, and my other life, one for which I desperately prayed for forgiveness. For as long as I can remember, I have known that there was something deeply colourful and tormenting between my legs, that this unnamed untamed thing stood in the way of my good Coptic girlhood. Starting with when I was ten, I could not help but cocoon with her every night and sink into all the colours and feelings she invited. When my mother found out, she taught me all the Orthodox things about *al 7itta illi ta7t,* "the place down there": this place, she insisted, was only for a future husband, for future children, for God, but certainly not for me. It was a delicate and forbidden place, a disgusting thing that I needed to forget about until it was time. So I named my thing down there, my forbidden, disgusting friend: *Lola.*

No matter how hard I tried, how many liturgies I prayed, how many Coptic hymns I sang, how many forced confessions I gave to the Orthodox priests, dutiful fasts, even hot tears of guilt, I always returned to Lola. And we cocooned together: guilty and curious, tormented and alive. Lola spoke a wordless language that did not bear the hostilities of my two first languages, Egyptian Arabic and English. She took me to places of rapturous joys without a passport. She let me wear my hair the way it naturally sprouted from my head: big, curly, frizzy and round, overtaking my face. She flushed my cheeks and rippled through all of my curves with the brightest and most delicious colours: unabashed, without condition, without being earned. She did not mind my poverty as an immigrant. Nor did she mind my unmoored in-between, having arrived young enough to forget my first language but not fully in command of my second in North America. Somehow, she held all my worlds together in that one place, that place down there, my forbidden, disgusting friend: Lola.

I was almost forty when I realized I didn't know the word for *vulva* in my first language. And I learned that the word for sex in my ancestral Coptic had become a swear word in *masry,* the Egyptian Arabic slang that Copts now speak after the Arab conquest of Egypt in the seventh century. *Nik. Fuck.* It made sense. Sex and sexuality are deeply repressed in both the diaspora and the homeland, drawing on an almost tragic intertwining of a patristic Orthodoxy and coloniality. The genealogies of *kapt,* sexual repression, is not just the result of being occupied by the British at the height of their Victorian era, but religious institutions that capitalized on the tight and narrow hold over pleasure, transitioning it from *haram* to *halal* on the whims of the most powerful. Whalebone corset not just around our hips, but a vice on our brains and vulvas too, all while a Eucharist burned in our mouths.

In the end, it was Lola who taught me:

I ~~was~~ am a good Coptic girl, no matter what they tell me.

My Vulva's name is Lola

أخيراً يا بنتي
akhiran ya benti.
at last, my good friend.

فينك من بدري
faynik min badri?
where have you been?

مستنياكي
mistaniyaki.
waiting for you.

The Choice of UnChoice.

No / لأ / ⲗⲁⲁⲩ

> *Listen O bride and lend your ear.*
> *Forsake your people and your father's home*
> *for your chastity has appealed to the bridegroom,*
> *and he is your husband.*
> *and to him you will submit.*
>
> *—a passage from the Coptic Rites of Crowing Ceremony*

+++

Over time, I realized that my love affair with Lola was a love story with consent. To choose. To say *yes* in myriad ways, sometimes shyly, quietly, and at other times resoundingly and brave so that joy and pleasure echoes off the walls—loud—as it contracts through my skin and through my life *here,* on this earth and alive. And to learn how *to* say no with grit and force, and to be honoured for it. This is also a story of a different sort of longing: to be a Coptic Orthodox woman who is worth more than her purity and submission to a man, whether he be father, uncle, male cousin, brother, bishop, priest, or husband. To be worth more than the hymen between my legs. To be a Coptic woman who desires. No shame or guilt. And while a classed and diasporic privilege has saved me from the Upper Egyptian public and bloodstained announcement of my chastity on my wedding night, the threat of that soaked bedsheet remained throughout most of my childhood, dangled close and public, just waiting . . . as I came into knowing Lola and into knowing myself.

It was the lessons of consent I learned through motherhood and a well-paired partnership that helped me to repair and transcend the sense of coercion and unchoice that I often felt in my Coptic life. Well into adulthood, I endured long worship services, long Lenten seasons that largely called for a vegan diet, and long periods of sexual abstinence against my own desires. Despite these coercions, I deeply loved the worship music, but I hated the words. I loved the smell of the incense on my clothes and in my hair, but I hated the devout comportment of standing to suffer, then suffering to stand. I stood throughout these services and in Sunday school lessons, regularly perched on the edge of hunger, or sleep, or a repressed desire *for something else.* And when I piped up about it, I was often quieted, or denied, or threatened by priests, parents, bishops, aunties, uncles, cousins, Sunday school teachers, choir leaders, spiritual mentors, and devout friends. They did not do this out of spite. Rather, they honestly feared for my afterlife, my roots, and more importantly, the honour of my Coptic girlhood, my Coptic womanhood, and then . . . my Coptic motherhood. Never mind the social combustion waiting on the other side of my wanting. Underlying such an ascetic way of life was a purity culture so deep that the only liberation was the destruction of my own hymen.

So, the universe coldly delivered:
I attended my cousin's wedding exactly ten days after I was raped.

✣✣✣

4:54 pm.
at that moment
the very last bit
of childhood
in me broke.
and, I don't know
if I chose it.

September 6, 2007
Personal Diary

✣✣✣

I'm afraid that one day someone will open up this book and discover
who I really am,
who Lola is.

afraid and
(un)afraid.
an almost dare.

that she slept with a man she barely knew. a man who was really a boy,
that in a sense she raped herself and set herself free.

now, no one owns me.
no one can.

I own myself. only God owns me.

he owns me beyond the scarring and the bruising.
beyond every rumbling mistake and the open cracks
bubbling and spitting up with childhood's anger.

the boy's colour was a shade darker than mine.
with a birthmark in the centre of him,
like a passing shadow.

a boy who served soy steamers
carrot cake and
chocolate cake.

a boy whose emotional disjunct was clear as day.

but somehow today, I wanted to see him and reconcile my anger
with him, to set the slate clear and cold grey. to set up the abandon.

but somehow, he clings, tentatively.
and the thought makes me shake
a little.

next time,
may there be a
little love, a
little understanding.
a bit of my old dream.

Yesterday I was distraught
by guilt's grief.

today I am determined
to survive myself.

I only let him hold my hand when we crossed streets.
and every time, he did just that.

I make him nervous.
(perhaps I should have been more nervous).

Afterwards, he cleaned up the bed, as if nothing happened,
a motion to hide the evidence and ease me back into reality.

Afterwards, I pretended everything was alright
though the numbness melted a little.
I cried in the shower, like a hiccup,
falling out by accident.

i cried to my best friend.

and I could not sleep.

today I am much better.

I will not let this
own me.

this was a choice of the unchoice.

the tug, the pull.
the trip and fall downwards

habibi.

time to get up.

September 10, 2007
Personal Diary

+++

So, a few hours ago, I lay down to take a nap;I felt so defeated. And in my head, I resolved: "God himself has to save me. purely. soundly. He has to be the one to save me from myself. from this."

And I'll confess that, during the entire weekend of my cousin's wedding festivities, I was ever so haunted by the beauty and the ugliness of what I've witness in myself.

And I felt myself slipping and slipping into something I didn't recognize.

And I hated myself. And loved myself and hated myself and loved myself.

"By the grace of God, I am who I am."

All of my ugliness and sadness, and cracking flaws belong to me. They are my beauty.

Even then, I have faith that God loves me. and desire me beyond them all.

Beneath all of this, I know there's a beautiful human being in me somewhere. She's just waiting to be set free.

She's coming out. Slowly. I can feel it. She's coming.

I deserve so much better than what I allot myself in the world.

I deserve so much better than I give myself and allow myself to take from the world.

I deserve a better experience than o

to love and to be loved.

I deserve a spiritual, intellectual, emotional, and sexual fit, so that being silent is not really being silent. And alone is not alone.

This revelation didn't hit me until I was sitting on the toilet in a Persian women's homemade salon. My cousin sat outside in the quiet bustle of bride-to-be buzz, and I cried.

And I realize that I was the one abusing myself. I was the one offering myself as a sacrifice to everything I was suffocated by, angered by, trapped by. I was burning myself first, before they could catch me and cage me in.

During my cousin's wedding, I itched to crawl outside my skin again.

"Son of orthodoxy to the daughter of orthodoxy by the life of orthodoxy . . . "

I wanted to scream.

Where's the Christianity in that? Where is Christ?

It's like in all orthodoxies, he just fell out and no one ever noticed.

And for some reason, I began to cry when they told my cousin that her body belonged to her husband now.

And then, as the abuna *was leaving, my father got up to talk to him, and I just wanted to run.*

All the well wishes for marriage made me want to cry. 3obalik.

I was so uncomfortable in my dress. And I rearranged the shawl over and over so it would cover up my gold strapless dress. I felt more naked at this wedding than lying under o.

i never want to do this. this wedding thing. at least today and this weekend. the whole process disillusions me.

i feel disillusioned by everything,

by church, my father, my work, love,

so now i know what I have to do.

i have to manage a quiet recovery.
I have to fall in love with myself again,
fall in love with my own company,
with my own particular strain of Christian faith,
with my work,
with my body.

no man can serve that to me.

September 17, 2007
Personal Diary

✢✢✢

Back then, when I still believed that I needed absolutions for my sins, I sat across a Coptic Orthodox priest and confessed to my own rape, looking for some sort of absolution to release the guilt. The date was September 18, 2007, just nine days after I had stripped the sheets off my bed with the hopes that laundry could undo memory and bloodstain in one swift cycle. And from under the leaden weight of shame, I admitted to the suffocating guilt that haunted my long and isolated walks, my disassociated and wide-eyed gaze out of the pews, a Coptic icon frozen in the stillness of another sort of death. I remember how the priest tentatively rolled the Coptic cross that Copts kiss, after they kiss his hands as an avatar of holiness thanks to his proximity to the Eucharist. He looked like he did not know what to say, whether to comfort or to scold. So I waited, one ticking second after the next, under his gaze. Finally, after a long pause, he replied:

Are you being suffocated, or are you the one suffocating yourself?

All I remember was the bitter taste of my suppressed gasp, incisor teeth gritting to the bottom of my locked jaw to quieten the stifled jump of my diaphragm. I held my breath like someone had just punched me. But he was right: without air, I could not cry. I sat with that question for over thirteen years. Rolled it under my tongue like a razor-sharp mousse, like the way he was rolling that cross. Rolled it in my ears on the subway. On walks. Over breakfast. While making dinner. In the shower. Behind my smiling eyes when meeting with my cousins and school friends. With the Coptic Eucharist hot in my mouth. And I heard that question in my quietest moments with Lola, when she too could not breathe. For a long time.

Then, one day I pulled out my diary and wrote a single sentence on a single page:

The choice of unchoice is still rape, habibi.

That day, I held my open diary in my hands. I took a deep breath, took in all the air that I could and . . . I finally cried.

Thirteen years. It took thirteen years to absolve myself and to breathe beyond the curse that Lola, that *desire* brought into my Orthodox world. It was the words of a good friend, a Coptic pastor who had converted into another denomination that held me through it, in a digital bear hug through that precarious but profound connection of a virtual friendship:

What does it say about a Church and a culture if the only liberation out of it is rape?

Something inside of me cracked open and finally let the relief in.

✢✢✢

I realize it now, almost three years to the day.
in the most loss of choice
I finally set myself just a little more free to choose.

and all the mishaps that followed were not mishaps at all,
but part of my life's story, a falling out of a Coptic constraining
that would have robbed me of choice anyway.

June 2, 2009
Personal Diary

✢✢✢

For Coptic women, whose agency over consent is overseen by a long line of men, saying *no* and saying *yes* to pleasure and desire is deeply fraught. The Coptic Orthodox Church does not believe in the concept of consent (Zacharia 2021). Rather, consent belongs to God as our bodies belong to God. And the gatekeepers to God are ascetic monks and bishops, all shaped and primed to be representatives of God on this earth, men who often and theoretically do not have sex, and who do not *want* themselves. While Coptic priests can marry, those who do marry and are publicly known not to consummate their marriages are celebrated in the community as modern-day saints, *better than us* for containing their desire in the face of a fellow pulsing body—often their wives—and saying *no* despite the permission of the holy contract of matrimony. I cannot help but think of the quiet of the night.

Are you being suffocated, or are you the one suffocating yourself?

In my long solitary walks, wrestling with memory and guilt, another question slipped in and regularly clipped at my toes: What does it say about Coptic girlhood if our belonging is contingent on our intact hymen, on a lifelong of *no*-ing as part of *self*-knowing? What does it also say about Coptic boyhood, whose own sexual repression—*kapt*—also has to reckon with a gendered authority on sex and consent that valorizes ascetic heroes who could not touch themselves without shame, who fought demonic apparitions in the form of women whose bodies look like their mothers', sisters', *tantes'*, and mine?

When I was just short of twenty, a young Eritrean Orthodox girl in my Church tragically died after suffering an aneurism in her fourth-grade classroom. My Upper Egyptian and devout father insisted we attend the funeral services to mourn with the family, drawing on the passage in Romans 12:15; if it takes a village to find joy, then it takes a village to mourn too. We could not leave our fellow parishioners to carry the burden of this sadness alone. So, we went to co-shoulder some of the heaviness despite not knowing her or her family personally.

Her tiny silver casket lay at the front end of the church, and I watched and wept as her family wept. Standing in the back of the women's section, I watched as Eritrean women held each other through thin white veils stained with grief, containing each other's bodies through the push and pull of heavy feeling. When it was time for a brief word, a working-class man stepped forward from the pews with a folded paper in his hand and nervously cleared his throat. But he was pre-empted by the local Coptic priest, who quickly stepped into the pulpit. This priest was a short, stocky ascetic-looking man with a long white beard. In his sermons, he regularly congratulated himself on being neither monk nor bishop, but simply a priest who *could* have married, but *didn't*, who could have had the prestige and praise of monkhood but *didn't*, all so he could devote himself to theological education, Coptic language revival, and pastoral service. He had a strident voice that often rang sharp, and one he could barely calibrate for somber occasions. With his eye on the little silver casket, his voice echoing off the walls, he loudly praised this little girl for timing her death, thanking God that she had died before "she was touched by a man."

When the words sunk in, I bit my lip to taste the blood this man was looking for.

Here. Happy?

After the service, I sat in my father's van, stunned. My tears would not stop. Between debilitating hiccups and thick gasps for air, all I could think was,

Is that all that matters? Is that why she *mattered, if at all? Is that why* we *matter?*

And I felt like I didn't matter at all. Not until a husband fucked me. Or I died beforehand, a virgin. And even then, after death, as I will lie disembodied, I will still be measured by the body I will be leaving behind, stranded in an eternity of an unreachable good Coptic girlhood for good.

Coptic Erotica.

Yes / أيوة / ⲁⲉⲓⲟⲁ

Almost twenty years after this little girl's funeral, I remember hovering over the words of Audre Lorde's 1978 "Uses of the Erotic" in a cafe and letting my fingers trace each page of her essay. I wanted all of her words to embrace me. I read each line slowly, chewing on words and meanings behind the constrictions building in my chest. In the solitude of my reading, I felt *seen* and my skin rippled with recognition.

> *. . . we have attempted to separate the spiritual and the erotic, thereby reducing the spiritual to a world of flattened affect, a world of the ascetic who aspires to feel nothing. But nothing is farther from the truth. For the ascetic position is one of the highest fear, the gravest immobility. The severe abstinence of the ascetic becomes the ruling obsession. And it is not one of self-discipline but of self-abnegation.*

Much of my Coptic life hinged on the word *no*; *no* animal products through lent, *no* jokes that are too crass, *no* short dresses, *no* lipstick before communion, *no* cleavage, *no* extra sleep on Sundays, absolutely *no* masturbation, *no* dancing, *no* "worldly" music, *no* sex before marriage, *no* kissing, *no* hugging, *no* touching, *no* laughing too loud, and other *nos*. There is even a term for all the *nos* in our life. Copts have a designated term in Egyptian Arabic: *bazl al-zat*, literally, experiencing joy *through* suffering and a staunch no-ing to desires. Just like Christ, who died on the cross for us, all with a smile on his proverbial God face. In other words, my spiritual belonging and joy often teetered on the thin edges of an abyss of wanting.

In this scarcity of *no*, I often asked myself: *What self will I reap here, in this hungry place?* What would it be like if my Coptic self hinged on the word *yes?* What if my Coptic life hinged on a lived and sensual *yes* that is not deferred to an afterlife, but one that is deeply vested in my living skin, in the here and now, and on self-knowledge that is not contingent on Coptic Bishops whose life is predicated on ascetic principals of *self-denial*, on a *no*. This reckoning began as the Covid pandemic's *no*s circled in: *no* contact. *no* proximity. *no* family. no *Church.* No *Copts* except for us—my partner and I, with our babies weaving in and out between our legs, grabbing us at our knobby knees.

In that most alone place, we streamed Orthodox services into our lonely kitchen, our bodies remembering the smell of the Church incense wafting under the aroma of home baked holy bread, *obran.* Hovering over a shared loaf, chewing on its warm goodness and the promise of life it contained within, we decided that we wanted to *live*. Looking down into our children's wide-eyed faces, we wanted them to live too. As my partner's loaves sang on the stove, crackling to settle after the burn of the oven, we decided to make good on the promise that the Egyptian word for bread—*'ayish* / عيش—implies: to eat bread is to *live.* And we decided to make good on the promise of the Eucharist too: to have faith is to imagine a life so possibly generous and abundant, that we and our children could bravely say *yes* to living, and to do so resoundingly. And that they could say *no* with grit and force and be honoured for it. Maybe in that resounding place of joy *and* pleasure, they would meet a kinder God—and co-sojourners in *this lived place* to keep them and grant them peace unto the end, wherever the end may be.

Those, O Lord, whose souls you have taken,
repose them in the paradise of joy, in the region of the living forever,
in the heavenly Jerusalem, in that place,
and we too, who are sojourners in this place, keep us in your faith,
and grant us your peace unto the end.

—The Priest, Commemoration of the saints, the Coptic Orthodox Liturgy

✢✢✢

The revolution has begun.

Or the idea planted.
Or the dare set out on the table. Like a dish. An invitation.
I'm just not sure yet if I will sit and eat.
If I will know how.

. . .

I realize how little I know compared to how much I want.
The gap is immense and between both ledges, desire and lava and darkness and demons,

but also new, and I hope, empowering lessons and experiences.
laying down the hauntings of
"what if," taking back what was taken from me.

Reparations.

And always, strangely with my body on the line.

once for my parents
then the church
then the husband
then al-nass (the people).

but now
for me.
just me.

April 19, 2022
Personal Diary

+++

when you are on the brink of your menopausing years, please promise me you will write a poem titled "soliloquy to a balding vagina" and dedicate it to natural women everywhere.

April 18, 2009
Personal Diary

+++

Oh *habibi,* I'm not going to do that. Not here, on the brink of middle adulthood.

How about I just rewrite the genesis story for her instead?

+++

Re-writing Eve.

I think Eve
fucked Adam
under the knowledge tree
and the apple was her vulva.
And that she. rode. him. hard.
frightening both man and God
of the promise and prowess
of womanhood.

coptic erotica

all holy partitions are clad in red.
red velvet curtains. red carpets.
the red *barashayn* sashes,
all the red roses.

but when you bleed, they throw you out.
containment of the first wanting.

uneasy conversions

if my Coptic hymen is
equal
one-to-one
to your Coptic
foreskin
why do we not sing more of the
circumcised
Christ?

why do we not pin
His foreskin
on the cross
and embed its meaning
into the folds and contours
of his Godhood?

why do we not
valorize
His cleanliness
and
His purity
as
it stands
contingent
on the
extra skin
between
His
legs?

Blooming

.   .   .

    .   .   .

        .   .   .

i. can't.
    not. yet.
(then when?)

i. don't. know.

> but I know the feel of slithering eyes beyond the red velvet curtains. recognizing the beginning of the dreaming: red flowers tucked into the tightest corners: Blooming.

wanting

in my new fantasies, I am on top.

I gather the thick fabric of collarbone in one hand, as I grip hair with the other.

and the entire world is in between my legs. gushing forward. contracting inward. wanting.

Reparations

Reparations
is to revenge fuck
through a long line of men
to heal a lineage of
ancestral women
whose only
recourse
was to
not
fuck
at
all.

coptic witch

with his face so closely
tucked into mine
in his grey, greens, and blues
he looked me dead in the eye
and whispered:

"you are magic"

And through all the breathing,
I could only purr and
shimmer in colour,
awed by the sacred alchemy
and healing
our naked bodies offered
us
both.

Crush.

Let's play emotional hide and go

seek

where i count to a number
not yet shared between us,

where I come to find you

in the slippages of
of our tense
cordiality.

in the stealth
of my hellos
and thank yous,

I wonder if you can see
how
my colours glimmer
open
and then shut,
partitioning like waves

I wonder if you can see
that my eyes are
a mirror portal
between the sea and sky of
all of my unspoken,
with the truth
so tightly contained
in the
underneath,

like flying shipwrecks.

A faith of abundance.

forget the eyeliner.
let him see the wrinkles. so he knows each crease
of how this flesh folds
so he knows
the imprints of the journey this body has taken
the babies this belly has carried. the stretched white line
marking their arrival
and your own survival.
so his mouth can follow the
the welled-up place where the tears linger before they spill
downwards
the crinkling of joy that etches upwards

forget the concealer
let the darkened shades underneath
sing as a testament
to the fatigue
of a liberation hard fought. and won.

take up space in his mouth.
  let him run his hands through your hair
  marking your gentle and slow transition as
  an ancestor in the making.

and let him fill you
  as you envelope him
he too looking for refuge. as the others have done
and you have so bravely given.

and will give again. and again. and again. and again. and
again. and again.

The Brave

the Brave
tastes metallic in my mouth
   a rush of silver
pluming upwards
   against the purple
kabooms of the Below.

when did those hidden and warm curls
grow their own heartbeats?

As I sit still to steady myself
   the Brave threatens to topple us both over.

You. Me.
         and a net of winged stars
   coerced and fidgety
      on my fingertips.

okay kiddo
my inner voice steadies
you've got this.

Do I?

I sink
      teeth leadened
into the tight corner of my cheek
and swallow past
a tongue parched into
   desert and sand.

hand on door.
   eyes muffling an inner gasp
then
   the click of the knob
         as it releases the lock
                                    forward.

Coptic Pussy

Abuna,
I'm going to make you real jealous
in confession.

Ready?

Between clasped palm and chaffed knee
I want you to know
that I orgasm in colour.

Vibrating pinks
ululating golds
and
flashing white tunnels
echoing directly to God

Diamond seas then
emerald fields
that waterfall
upright.

And
every time I crest those waves

I am not sorry.

Rather, in the
Oh-my-Lord
of my coital travels

I pray
with clasped palm and chaffed knee
thanking God
for the Coptic pussy
I got.

Re-Birth

he insisted to kiss the scar
hidden between belly and vulva
a torn gate
through which,
one by one,
my children
were deftly pulled
into this world.

it is my first artifact of motherhood
white and tight.
and his mouth traced this line tenderly,
his fingers
pulling back the puckered bits of belly
i have often hidden in shame
and neglect.

for the first time
i let the scar sink
into someone's mouth.
i closed my eyes
and let the blue red pain
of this passage
pass over me
as i barter memory for pleasure
flashback for orgasm
contracting in reds
and the gasping sight of a small black iris
blinking in disbelief,
tiny hands reaching out
frantic and searching.
mama?

as his mouth trailed
the map of stretchmarks fanning
across my belly
I could not help but
reckon with the
the raw and concomitant act of
sex and birth,
pain and pleasure,
death and life.

Coptic Porn Star

I want to be your Coptic porn star.

I want to show you
my inner red velvet
golden censers
steaming with incense.

I want to get down to my knees
and confess
to all the things
you have already
written on my body
as it shifts
as it moves
as it lives
as it bleeds

and as it heals from birth.

I want to be your Eve
pomegranate jewels
between the legs

your mary magdalene
catching your first
cast stone
between the teeth.

I want to be your temptress
in the desert
and in your holy books

bringing the monks
down to their knees
to confess
to me.

sharmouta | whore

I wonder
if that's the word
the Orthobros
will use
when they know the full story

when they read the words

of a
kapt
liberated

of a
life
desiring and lived out loud.

sharmouta | whore.

Even
the most devout
of Coptic women,
girls, and nuns

who tucked only piety in their voice
have been accused:

sharmouta | whore

for daring to
to sing
the words and teachings of
a pure and reverent Christ.

I am beginning to wonder

if they are mixing up the words

whore for cantor, *sharmouta* for singer

and I cannot help but ask: what kind of kink is that?

Nafas | to breathe

of all things
I simply want to

to settle
my ear
on the pulse
and breathe

in
and
out

then

out
and
in

wordless
and silent.

until the restlessness begins

and we crawl into the
recluse
again.

Nifs | to desire

come breathe with me
sink your self
against my self
and pour your breath into my breath
so that both our lungs
may contract
and touch
through the
skin.

Nifsi | I desire

for Marcus

nafas, to breath and to be.
nifs, to desire.
nifsi, I desire.

nafas, nifs, and nifsi
is a funny sequence of Arabic words
like disjointed siblings.
strung together they
slide off my tongue
like a gentle kiss
on the lips,
mouth against mouth
breath into breath.
realizing as I say it
that

to breathe a self into my desire
is my desire breathing a self
back into me

كان نفسي أتنفس زي كدة من زمان

I have longed for this self
to breathe into me like this
for always.

(and with you

I am finally

breathing.)

Abound.

for each other

what if
in the end
we are both the gods and the saints
and our holy ablutions are the rise and crest
of our bodies into one another,
a communion of another sort.

Our body Our blood Our holy spirit.

what if we
exile all clerical mediators
from between our legs
and instead
sink our own fingers
into the divine partitions
of things seen and unseen.

so that
we too, having sufficiency in everything
may abound
in every good deed?

VI.

Coptic Sex in a Series

Sex in Arabic

Sex in Arabic
is like slipping into the familiar
bends of our spoken calligraphy

lines slurred and elided
into a twisty embrace
dots above and below
all intricately
intertwined

with the meanings between us
sometimes hushed
like a secret
and sometimes
loud and gasping
like the curls falling out of our heads

Sex in English

Sex in English
is a borrowed joy,
a voyeur
into
a second skin
that is
home
and
not
home
all at
once.

Sex in Coptic

Sex
in Coptic
is a muted
desire
for the things
that once
were
but will
never
be
Of ancestral burdens
having to
steal whimpered intimacies
from the exotic
embrace of faded manuscripts,
all while
eyeing the size of
our ruby areolas
and wondering
if they can
be carried
off
in the mouth.

VII.

here, in diaspora.

Here.

Sometimes I use an app to help me focus on my work, one that pairs me with others somewhere around the world, also looking to co-beat distractions and work, a focus-share app if you will. And for the first time today, I was paired with another Egyptian woman named Omnia.

I loved the look of surprise on her face when I correctly pronounced her name. She asked me if I was Egyptian and when I said yes, she said: "You don't look Egyptian." So I flipped into Arabic, almost to prove it to her, growing just a wee self-conscious of its broken edges and yet, how closely it also passes for homegrown.

But she insisted: "Your Arabic is great, but the language coming out of your mouth doesn't match your face."

I held my curls up to her like an offering. Look at me, *I wanted to say.* See me.

But instead, I explained that I was a diaspora child and that I regained my Arabic back like a lost limb, thanks to my partner, my cousins, my tayta, and my return to Egypt. Thanks to my own labours too.

Then at a meeting at work, a Black colleague used me as an example of "passing" and said:

"Sorry to use you as an example, but if it wasn't for your hair, you look very Italian."

I laughed and looked into my zoom image again and again, and sunk my fingers into my own hair. The proof's in the pudding, kiddo.

Then I realized why I so deeply want to be held. Because so badly, I want to belong. And with a naked body on the line, who can refute such human belonging, even if it is momentary and contingent and fleeting.

But for a moment, it does not matter.
And, even when it does, I will take it.
I will take it.

February 27, 2023
Personal Diary

✣✣✣

immigrant settler in diaspora

there is a strange confidence in planting your feet in a place

and daring to imagine
            and to believe
                        i belong here.
                        this is my place.
                        i belong to this place. here.

I'm no longer a guest. Just elbows and hair, edging my way into this story.

> *It is mine too. All of it. The smooth bends and the jagged edges.*

Gutting my home was an inadvertent invitation to my ancestors.
Gutting my ancestors was an inadvertent invitation to our inherited wrath.

Wringing their hands, our ancestors asked: *what will we give our babies after all that they have taken from us?* They paced. They sang. They baked. They hoped memory would be enough. *Let them follow the wealth they have taken from us. They will fight for us.*

Wringing our hands, we ask: *what will we give our babies after our ancestors have been taken from us, carted away in ideological coffins, gutted and smuggled to keep diaspora pews warm and the American red funded?*

And so here we are, first generation and guests no longer.

Just elbows and hair, edging our way into this story.

Little Egyptian Drag King.

إنتِ تتفكّي بخمَس رجّالة

"when they break you, they will find five men"—

—Baba to me at fourteen. and always thereafter.

the shift starts at four when we all pack into the red van. sit like guests among disheveled mops. gaping buckets. and clinking cans of clean.

then the roundup. each one with their own folding chair in the back. the silent drive.

Before I leave the van, I am already feeling the grasping motion of the towel wiping down the tables under my fingertips. the gentle hum of the vacuum,
up down up up down up up down.
the buzzing against my open palm. the endless hallways stacked side by side like toys.

with each tumbling crumb, I flash back to what the room holds during the day. To the smells that trace the tables. the sounds that layered their tops with memory, instructions, conversations, lunch.

Then the kitchen. Replacing the garbage bags beckons an escape into my ears. and from my ears, to somewhere else. an auditory teleporting as hands tie plastic into strings and strings into tight relentless knots. the cracking of bones.

I love the peel of the clean garbage bags, bellowing as they catch the air. that final swipe before the confining. empty.

Then the mop. The dive. that squeeze. the mane threading out in a large fan to sway from side to side. Without dark ringlets, I imagine this is how a white girl's hair moves. Lift, drag, follow, sway. Even the mops, with their thin frames, look somehow effortless.

But I am something else. I am my father's man. I am his eldest son. short and square.
I am the man of my men's men. steel my jaw to each bump and bruise, scaffolding silence upon silence to look up. hold a gaze. avert another. translate, unshaken, between hostile tongues. Barter between uneven worlds.

that deep breath after, the expanding of rib cage under contracting skin. twitching heart. convulsing lung.

Back to the vacuum. An exquisite hum:
up down up up down up down up up down.
I am my father's right-hand man.
أتفَكّ بخَمَس رجّالة

On faith and breaking cycles of intergenerational trauma

when my babies ask me if I believe

I say

on most days
I believe in a God
but not the one I inherited

Instead, I believe in
a universe so abundant and kind

that heaven is a place
where our once powerless taytas
have somehow partnered with the Divine

and together
they pull the levers from the Beyond

to cheer us on as

we redirect
course

and break cycles of
intergenerational trauma
in their holy name.

ancestral friendshipping

i live on Anishinaabe territory
unceded and unyielding
on this land so called "canada"
and
sometimes I wonder
what my tayta
would say to her Anishinaabe neighbour

أعملّك قهوة؟
May I make you coffee?

I think she would make the coffee
and sit quiet and shy
as Saidi taytas do
waiting to politely ask

أجاملك إزاي؟
how may I return this gift back to you,
the way your land
has held
the stories
of my kin
and made
enough room
to take them in?

She would brew the coffee
with the best cardamom and liquorice spice
she would sweeten it
to cut the bitter edge
and watch the foam pucker
and rise to a perfect pitch
then pass it over tenderly
with ground coffee
still on her fingertips.

بالهنا والشِّفا
with pleasure, she would say,
and with this bittersweet joy of repair between us.
for in these times, we are all we have.

and sit quiet and shy
as Upper Egyptian taytas do.

Academic Karens

Academic Karens
are so polite
all smiles and eyes
of strategic oblivion
that makes their hearts
sing
of equity diversity and
inclusion.

they pat their own backs
as they hum along
and
watch
you bleed
from the
thousand and one
gentle
cuts they've
measured
across your body.

Sorry.

And after you write about it
they look to you
all whimper and tears:

Did you cite me?

Progressive Fragilities.

With progressive white supremacy
you have to decide
on your feet
and with your
life hanging
between your hands
whether to massage their EDI vanity

Or

just with your eyes
judge their intentions
and
play chicken
with their unsaid
fragilities

all. while. smiling.

and

staying open for their punch.

We Are the Children of the Sun

for my Ns

I write this to you in the year an officer stepped on George Floyd's neck for 8:43 minutes and murdered him.
After hearing the news, you turned to me and asked:
"Will an officer stand on my neck because I am brown?"

At six, it was the year we had to begin.

Egyptians come in all shades and shadows, and the Egyptian colloquial Arabic is rich in capturing the beauty of our changing skin. In Canada, our colours are all the more striking, as our skin pays homage to the sun when it sleeps. In the winter, our skin remembers and it waits.

 # SayTheirNames # BlackLivesMatter

+++

Ya Habibi | يا حبيبي
We are the Children of the Sun
When it sees our skin, it kisses it and says "Hey, do you remember me?"

Remember my body where you used to live?
This is your first home.
I cooked you in here. I danced with you here.
And I loved you here from the very beginning.
What colour is your first home? It is the colour of Mama.
And of you.

In the winter, our skin is like شاي باللبن | *shay-bel-laban,*
tea sweetened with milk and honey.
It is the colour of slumbering wheat, قمحاويين | *amḥawi.*
In the winter, our skin sleeps. But it always remembers:
We are the Children of the Sun.

Remember my arms where you used to sing?
This is your second home.
I rocked you here. I fed you here. And I sang to you here,
from the very beginning.
What colour is your second home? It is the colour of Mama.
And of you.

In the summer, our skin remembers.
When it sees the sun, it sings.
We are the colour of عسل أبيض | *'asal abyad* and then عسل إسود |
'asal iswed, wild honey that simmers into dark molasses.

We are the children of the sun,
and our skin comes in many shades and shadows:
amber, maple, and toasted sesame.

We are
مسمسمين | *misamsimin* like a sweet sesame stick
معسلين | *mi'asilin* like glistening honey
أمحويين | *amḥawin* like the gold of full grown wheat
بِيض | *bied,* like the white of cotton and clouds.
سُمر | *sumr,* black like the rich silt of the Nile that feeds us all.

We are all Children of the Sun.
When it sees our skin, it kisses it and says
"Do you remember me?"
And our skin whispers back: "I do."

escharpe comrades.

for Mariam

it is a gift to find each other
on the other side of the veil

thinking back
to church bench strandings
when our collective
curls were tucked into the straight and narrow
eyes pinned ahead to the
ostrich egg.

sali | Pray.

I would have never thought
there could be life
beyond this
when
legs were dutifully crossed
and
lips pressed, closed and clean.

sali | Pray.

i *did* pray.
I prayed
to imagine
a gentle coiling of these curls
beyond this
escharpe.
I prayed to
to desire more
than just
enough.

i prayed to be both seen and unseen.
to be made holy while unholy.
legs closed *and* wide apart.

sali | Pray.

It is a gift to find each other
on the other side of the veil

the Pacific

to stand in front of the boundless ocean
is to feel bound
tooth and nail
into skin and bone.

balacona baptisms

for Miray

a chosen family
is made through the grit and spit of
sunflower *'azzazza*
on a high Toronto balcony,

all the discarded shells
a meaty metaphor
for the previous lives we have lived
and the masks we've shed
to make it to
here.

countless cups of tea
come and go
and
between the sweet and salty
of watermelon and seeds,
our alternate kinship
is made as we are
pinching with the
the gossip
of who said what to whom.

When the rain comes in, sudden, heavy, and sideways,
we do not care that we are drenched, instead we
greet this storm of
holy ghost and urban *myron*
as a *balacona* baptism,
a promise of a life well lived, *together*,
and a redemption of all that is possible and joyous.

Combustible

run, kiddo.
hop onto your bike and run

run towards the sun. or away.
but just run

on your feet. on your heels
let them sink in
and leave a trail behind

wind.
fire.
spit.
gas.

be combustible
be angry.
be ugly.

or just
be quiet.

let your eyes do the talking.

let silence sit next to you like
your armoured shadow.

savour in the discomfort
it begets.

connect. covert and tight
to all the hidden delicious.

relish in the relishing.

and reject
all that does not bring you joy.

just run, kiddo.
hop onto your bike and run.

My Fat Bike's Name is Also Lola

this friend
of steel and bone
daily suspends my frame
on a single ledge

like I was made of feather and air

and together we ride. everywhere.

past the past
past the cornfield of hilton, ny
past the retro edges of the toronto burbs
past the bulk and grit of Greece, NY

past the past and into here.

speed 2
gear 6
sometimes 7
so the delicious burn spreads

then builds.

a thin breeze to kiss the forehead
the look over the left shoulder
then a smiley sink
into a most natural rhythm

of push and pull

forward.

Coptic Self-eldering

Coptic
self-eldering
is mostly quiet
frantic
sips of tea
while
gazing into an unknown
horizon

hoping and wishing
for ancestral insight
from the other side

all while
trusting deeply
that the joy on this end
threads through to the next
without the martyred anguish
they convinced us
was the only ticket
to walking
into the light

On the Politics of Civility (or Turning 40).

I peel her back
bit by bit
so she can finally find
her ease
and settle into the crass
of the most honest kind of living
desiring out loud
disdaining out load
reckoning out loud

clawing back all of the in/audibilities
of living
that were consistently
silenced

to be polite.
to be devout.
to be desired.

As perimenopause
unravels me curl
by curl
I think

of a liberation
often won with aging

of falling out of someone else's gaze

and sinking ever so softly
and smiling
into my own.

hope

hope
nips at my feet
like a
baby lion
as i eye
its arc
knowing
one day
it will
grow large enough
to devour
me

as its whiskers
kiss my toes
i think of
what it is
to be swallowed
whole
by the promise of
something Better,
if being enveloped
by ribs and cage
is kinder
than the dour
chains
of
not
having
hope
at
all.

3aysh | عيش | Life

for Marcus

when we pray
give us this day our daily bread
I imagine
that we pray
not to be held ransom
by hunger
but for memory to sustain us
when the bread basket is
empty
and for the faith
of knowing
that the next loaf
is coming.

reverse baptism

the way he slipped his finger into your mouth
and held you close
never minding the baptismal font of
blood between your legs
is something
your own ancestors
won't forget.

Un/Churched.

i fell out of Church
when they told me
that Jesus
hated the queers
and was so troubled
by the thought
of my pulsing
vulva
that
He was the
one who
cast
the first
stone.

a Coptic *taslīm* in Diaspora

It is strange to sink
into all that was forbidden.

the tight
the narrow
the wide
and the deep.

all while remembering the weight of the chains
of an interlinked transmission. *taslīm.*
hand after hand after hand
of sexual discipline. denial. and trauma. *al-kapt.*

all while embedded in the sweet
contractions of being human.

to finally let it all go.
and to fly.

A holy communion.

I am not your fucking *orbana*.

I am not your body of Christ
to be folded over
pulled
and broken
into crumbs
for you to consume me

only to pass me the remaining morsels.

I'm not your *kanisa*.

I'm not your virginal womb. or your *shuriyya*.

I am not your Virgin.
I am not your Eve.

I am not your hymen.

I am not your adulterous trope
as I desire to live beyond
the confines of what's between my legs
and as I live deeply there
in the intimate folds
of my Coptic vulva.

I am not your repentant Mary Magdalene.

I am not your *tasoni*.

I am not your homeland.

I am not your body.

I am not yours.

I partake of my own holy body and of my own holy blood.

In the name of Jesus Christ. Amen.

A love letter to Coptic girls everywhere

i believe you.

and no Jesus anywhere

would justify

the theological trapeze

and saintly decorum

of the regular violence

quietly dealt

to our tender skin.

when they tell you that bruises will better contour your faith,

don't believe them.

when they tell you to *endure*

the lashings of broken men

and to bear your cross,

remind them

that even Jesus

turned tables over

in the holy temple of God,

and you ask them:

what of our holy temple too?

A love Letter to Coptic orthobros everywhere

for my boys. always

in a world
doubled over as a furnace
of fire and brimstone

in which only broken bodies
are sacrosanct enough
to be holy,

even you must be broken too.

in the collective grief of witnessing your containment
and with
the warm imprint of
my sons' bodies on my arms

I write a new Coptic world

in which Coptic boys do not need to be
broken

in order to be made
into
holy men

I write a new Coptic world

in which Coptic boys are
already imbued with the
divinity
promised
to them
by
simply
being wholly
human.

VIII.

A New Taslīm

A Coptic Liturgy In the Basement.

Egypt's indigenous Copts sing their stories.

We meet each other in the Coptic Orthodox liturgy, for we have inherited this rite as the sung labour of the people. It is often here, in this sounded place, that we come to know our place in the world in a kind of collective knowledge-making through song. And we all must depend on each other to fulfill the liturgy's promise to pull heaven momentarily down to earth and be in physical and spiritual communion with God and with each other. It is in this act that we momentarily achieve a lived death to *hear* heaven. For us, heaven is a sound, a place of eternal *tasbīḥ,* or sung praise to God in the embrace of the heavenly saints, our family, our kin, and our ancestors. As the congregation, or the *sha'b,* we look to the priest, *abuna,* our father, to shepherd us through the most sacred parts of this holy communion, and it is the all-male cantors or *shamamsa* who set the pace. Finally, it is in the act of singing *together* that we forge the permissible public intimacies so deeply regulated in our community.

We sing to restore ourselves, to restore our place in the world, and one day, to restore our place in the beyond. In diaspora, this labour takes on an additional dimension, given the distance from the Egyptian homeland: the liturgy is where we have learned how to sing *home*. It is in these very hymns and spiritual songs where we also re-meet our kin long gone before us "*—as it was, and shall be, from generation to generation and unto the ages of all ages. Amen.*"

Yet this most holy place is fraught too. In its collective labour is a collective pain, a sonic inheritance of exile, first as a religious minority in our homeland, then as we immigrate to a new home, and finally as we exile from ourselves as Coptic immigrant girls. When we leave as children, we do not understand why the Egyptian Arabic is evaporating out of our mouths. We can only watch its vapours as it dances off of our lips. Similarly, as our bodies change and shift—with the arrival of our first periods that exclude us from the holy altars of our churches, with the birth of children and the baptismal absolutions to purify us from the very blood that made this life possible—we recognize our shift into a gendered and exiled minority *within* an exiled minority.

When I sing the liturgy, I am back in all the church basements I have ever been. Each of these soundscapes come back together, sonorous with the overlapping chatter, dishes, *alḥan*, whispers, debates, laughter, smiles, and *taranīm*—a rich tapestry of Coptic girlhood buzzing directly in my ears. It is not a soundscape I often bear with ease, because I often have to wrestle with the concomitant rush of grief and joy, loss and liberation, loneliness and that precious feeling of being held by everyone you know, and everyone who had a hand in raising you.

I left the Orthodox Church gradually, recognizing that I could not fully hold my children in their fullness in this place. And when the Covid-19 pandemic's isolation officially relegated us to virtual churches, I finally had the chance to reckon with its damage in the quiet of the pandemic's social exile. Surrounded by a new set of kin, many of whom are also Coptic outliers like me, I finally had enough courage to imagine an afterlife more abundant than everlasting, a Divine more forgiving than omnipotent, and a liturgy more reparative than repentant. And when Marcus began to worship in the basement, often virtually with other trusted kin, I would avoid the service, but my ears would strain to hear the liturgy leaking through the floorboards, to trace the sonic breadcrumbs home, to find the pulse of my own singing body.

One day I finally had enough courage to join them.
Together we prayed.
Together we began to heal.
And together we repaired.

+++

To go back to that space, I have to take a gummy. Something to take the edge off, ease the sharp edges of the Return. Sometimes wine. Sometimes a deep fatigue is enough, the memory of my boys still imprinted on my hips. Sometimes it is the memory of the Plague. Close and far. In and outside of our bodies.

All I know is that I go. I return. I take another gummy. Then I go back. Again.

In that space, I am strangely open in ways that I could have never imagined. I break bread with M. His bread. Our hands on each edge rewrite parts of our past anew. M sings. And I sit against his buzzing body. P breathes a warm light along the passages we have always known, easing some of the edges, but at times illuminating the jagged ledge of a steep cliff. A memory floats to the top, then settles again, shoved gently under the wine. Under M's voice.

This place is warm and whole. And bright. And full. The first time, I got to hold a world in which Tayta is back in her pew, sitting two to the front and one to the right. Sometimes to the left.

Mama always to my left, until I got older and switched to the right. One seat closer to the door. My maternal aunt is one pew in front of Mama, but one pew behind Tayta. The sequence of an unfulfilled matriarchy. We stand in order, the daughters behind the daughters. And the daughters behind the sons.

They all look alike, don't they?
Who wore the beard best, do you think? Jesus? Or T?
Maybe Abuna.
I don't know.
They all look alike to me now.

Another tante, *a family friend, files in behind us with her daughter, a happy bright beautiful girl (We still share virtual whispers of this place.* Al-kanīsa *and the ruptures with our mothers.)*

Then another tante *comes, her daughter in tow, eyes to the floor.*

They stand next to maternal cousins. Another family. Another sequence that cascades sideways. Cousins next to cousins. Sisters next to sisters.

In this basement place, I get to hold Tante *M, now gone from this world, she and her pineapple upside down cake. Her giggling high voice as she threaded my upper lip in the first painful rips of womanhood. Hair after hair. Red beating skin under her rubbing fingers.*

I had so many mothers there.

I loved it there. I hated it there.

I don't know.

The next day, my sober memory returns. Between the velvet folds of the warm, there are the muted traces of the Dark. The tightness. The eyes. The Silencing. The discipline. The boredom. The yelling. The wish over and over for the pew to split open, and take me below, back to my bed. To the warm.

Do we want to go back there? That tormented place?
(Do we bury ourselves again?)

When I take the gummy, a certain euphoria returns. The songs and hymns are mine again. Not the words, but the melodies. The ease with which they fit into my mouth. I want to take them all back. To take the me in them back. But there was so much pain in them too. Mama taught me to hide the pain. All the yelling. She cried and cried. I cried and cried to help her hide it and to shoulder some of this immigrant grief with her.

We sang. Together.
Side by side. Every Sunday like clockwork.
Daughters of Daughters.
Daughters of Fathers.

Why are we back here again?

I don't know. I'm sorry, but I don't know. Did we ever leave in the first place?

Have we been stuck here the whole time?

In the daylight, the protection returns. Older me tucks younger me under her arm.

We've got this. *I got you. Our matriarchy has begun. Not sideways or backwards. but Up.*

The prospect of this place, in the beyond, *feels like a close dance on a knife's edge. A clenched fist that may bloom into an open palm.* Is this what forgiveness feels like? I don't know.

Then I remember: the dark roundness of the tunnel downwards. Where the church is a full circle and there are no doors. Dark. And spinning.

But then this *space in the basement is hidden. Far and secret. And warm.*

I got out. We got out. Right? Do we want to wonder back out there, alone into the woods? Down into the spinning? Down to the Dark?

We are not alone. You are not alone there. M is there. P is there. Now D. Then another M.

And more are coming.

I *am there, in my entire fullness.*

Remember when you were looking for the Finding? Then you found yourself.

When you find the Finding, it spreads.

Undated, 2020,
Personal Diary
in the thick of the pandemic.

+++

A Coptic Liturgy for the un/Churched.

Gathering and Offertory

Let us bake this ancestral loaf of
عيش شمسي
sun bread of our grandmothers
a communion of bread dipped in oil
laced with salt and fava beans, *fūl*

Let's imagine
the *mulukhiya* that will drown it under a thick film of *samna*
and toasted coriander seeds.

Let us ponder the broth it will take to soften this bread
when it hardens:
life after death when
death hardens life.

Let us spin *life* from this dough and give birth to عيش. Bread.

Let us imprint our interlocking hands gently on its waiting face
leaving our fingerprints in its puckered roundness as it rises
again and again.

Remember, O Lord those who have brought unto You these gifts,
those on whose behalf they have been brought, and those by whom
they have been brought.
Give them all the heavenly reward. In this place. In this here.
And in this now.

Deferral unto death is thievery.
For we are not thieves of life. We are life itself.

هللويا. هذا هو اليوم الذي صنعه الرب
فلنفرح ونبتهج فيه
يا رب خلصنا، يا رب سهل سبلنا .
مبارك الآتي باسم الرب، هللويا.

Prayer of Thanksgiving

Peace is here. Peace is in our spirit.

We thank God for the smallest to the largest, for what is hidden within ourselves, and for what is visible from worlds beyond our own, *for every condition, concerning every condition, and in every condition.* For in God, there is hope, there is kindness, there is refuge, there is compassion, and there is endurance to bring us from this hour and to the next.

We ask and entreat you, O God, to help us find goodness in ourselves and in each other, to make each day holy, and to remember that we are always in the presence of the Divine, that we too are Divine.

May the confinement of our darkness never close in.
May our demons never win.
Take them away from us, from our families,
from our tables, from in-between our legs,
from our holy places.

But those things which are profitable, do provide for us, O God. By grace, compassion, and love of all the Prophets and Prophetesses who have whispered to us through the ages. Reminding us of our truths.

Amen. Lord have mercy (3).

The Absolution of Ministers

We now know that
the first sin came in the writing of the first sin. When Eve
dared to ask a question.
When she consumed before being consumed.

We now know that
the second sin came when the ministers convinced us it was
true.
As it was, and shall be,
from generation to generation,
and unto the ages of all ages. Amen.

Absolution will not absolve their broken books
nor absolve the broken bodies littered at the base of their
knowledge tree.

We pray that *the ministers of the day, the hegemons, the priests, the deacons, the clergy and their weak selves* not be absolved. That they may be held accountable. That they may reckon and be reckoned with *from generation to generation, and unto the ages of all ages. Amen.*

(First Reading, Trisagion hymn, Gospel)

*The Creed**

We *believe in God, who created all things good and all people holy.*

We *believe in Jesus Christ, God's beloved who came to earth to dwell among us. He was born into a nonconventional family who adored Him even when they did not understand Him. He challenged those in authority, proclaimed good news to the captives and set the oppressed free. For this, he was crucified, died and was buried. On the third day, he rose again and ascended into Beauty, raising all bodies, proclaiming us sacred.*

We *believe in the Holy Spirit, She who danced over the waters before time, whose wisdom resounds through the universe, who gives us word, prophecy, and vision.*

We are *knitted into the sacred tapestry of humanity, in communion with* each other in *all colours and genders.*

We are loved. *Not for doing or earning, but for breathing and being.* Our bodies are *sacred, rising and aligning, again and again, in this place. In this here. And in this now to everlasting life. Amen*

* This creed was written by M Ghaly who has kindly given me permission to include here.

The Anaphora / The Great Thanksgiving

Lift up your hearts. They are with the Lord.
Let us revisit the knowledge tree to pick up our ancestral scatters, leftover hearts, the breathlessness of leftover lungs.
Little Gods who died little deaths.
Let us bring them close. Let us sit among their remains *with Your Spirit* and mark our bodies with their ashes before we must go and plant another knowledge tree.

Let us give thanks to the Lord. It is meet and right.
Let us lean in and press our ears to the ground. And listen, imbued with gratitude, at the fleshy morsels memory has delivered to us. Let us trace the names of the ancestors we remember. and let us imagine those we cannot.
Let us find one another.
And remember we are not scavengers of life, but gardeners.
For we are not thieves of life. We are life itself.

We thank the Lord for this cracked earth; for the bleeding that began to water the roots; for the labour to come; for the labours of finding one another.

Meet and right, meet and right, truly, indeed, it is meet and right. God of truth, being before the ages and reigning forever, who dwells in the highest and looks upon the lowly, who has created the heaven, the earth, the sea, and all that lies therein.

By whom you have created all things, seen and unseen.

We pray that you see us.
We pray that our parents see us.
We pray that our children see us.
We pray that their children come and find us when we are but flowers at the base of their knowledge tree.

The Consecration

Let us recognize that all are already consecrated
And challenge the desecration of any body that overpowers another body.
Let us desecrate all that is considered holy, so that *all is holy*.
Let us peel away
the Orthodox in us
that excludes
In the name of Jesus Christ.
In the name of the other gods and prophets
In each other's name.
Amen.

dear God, grant us peace when we have to hold our piece for peace
grant us peace in the quiet labour of unlearning
as we remake and rewrite our worlds anew
as we parent ourselves the way we wish we were parented
as we parent our children, planting our love in them for this generation and the generation to come.

Dear God, grant us peace as we break cycles of generational trauma.
Grant us peace as we are evicted from our families. In thought and in spirit. And in the flesh.
Grant as peace as we are haunted in the mouth, tasting meals that made our mouths leap with joy
and our ears and hearts bleed with grief.
Grant us peace as we are exiled from our bodies,
and as we return.
Grant us the strength to make amends with those who hurt us, because they too are mending their own hurts.

Grant us peace as our world broadens to make room for worlds different from our own. As we expand beyond the ribs of Adam, growing into the full bodies of our shared humanity. Grant us peace with our selves. As we grow young and then grow old. As we transition from one dimension of ourselves into another. So that in each of these we find the Divine in all things. And we find the Divine in ourselves and in each other.

In the rivers and watersheds,
the soil and the air,
and every plant, grant abundance to the fruits of the earth,
for the poor among your people, for the widows, for the orphans, for the strangers, and for the labourers in every place,
and for the sake of us all, who entreat You and seek Your Holy Name.
For the eyes of everyone wait upon You, for You give them their food in due season.

Deal with us according to Your goodness, O You Who gives food to all flesh.

Fill our hearts with joy and gladness, that we too having sufficiency in everything always, may abound in every good deed.

May we always abound.
May we always abound.
May we always abound.

Commemorations

We commemorate all of those forgotten in our
commemorations.
We pray for the courage to ask why they were forgotten
and to remember those dis-membered
for their courage.
We ask the saints to kneel
so that transgressing and transgressed bodies can rise. So that
we may set each other free.
We pray for strength to follow these stories, to listen to them,
and restore their dignity.
We pray for patience in burdened silences. And to be kind.
We pray for strength to hold each other's confessions. And to
absolve our own.

Ⲭⲉ ⲛⲁⲓ ⲛⲁⲛ, Ⲭⲉ ⲛⲁⲓ ⲛⲁⲛ, Ⲭⲉ ⲛⲁⲓ ⲛⲁⲛ.
إرحمنا، إرحمنا، إرحمنا
Lord have mercy on us.
Let us have mercy on ourselves.

Fraction prayer for our daughters and for our sons

We are worthy to stand up in this holy place, the daughters *and* the sons.
We are worthy.

We are the Body.
We *are* the Blood.

Let us give thanks for knowing our place among the Gods.
God, who dwells among the lowly, made us seen and unseen, audible, gasping in our joy and pleasure, incomprehensible, infinite, eternal and finite
who made us queer, deep, and wanting.

You gave us your Body and Blood to live through. Let them hear your voice saying, "They who eat my Body and drink my Blood abide in Me, and I in Them." (John 6:56).

May we always abide.

Communion

Take eat of it, all of you, for this is our shared Body.
Take, drink of it, all of you, for this is our Blood.

Let us be the smiling mouths that fall into other smiling mouths
let us sink our bodies into one another. Embracing each fold warmly
as cocoons for each other's souls.

Let us each look eye into unblinking eye as we
reach for the most tender skin of hands
grasping for other hands.

Let us sit side by side in each other's journeys so that we may
never again travel alone, sharing morsels of this bread of life.

Take food of it, all of you, for this is our shared Body.
Take drink of it, all of you, for this is our Blood.

Never again shall any blood be made more precious, more
pure, or more whole, than another. Never again shall we part
our bodies, one from another.
Never again shall gender define us.
Never again shall who we love define us.

Never again shall nation define us.
In this life and in the next.

Never again shall another body desecrate another body.
Never again shall another body desecrate another body.
Never again shall another body desecrate another body.

Amen.

Afterword

The first time I let my curls go wild, I was on a small farm in Tennessee. I had come for a summer writing residency, trading rent for labour—spreading dry feed for the chickens at sunrise, barreling hay for the goats at dusk. It was the early months of Covid, and beyond the fences of that quiet expanse, my world was coming undone.

That summer, George Floyd's murder sent my community into the streets, a racial reckoning unfurling across America. Soon after, Sarah Hegazi, the Egyptian queer activist who was jailed, tortured, and fled to Canada on asylum, took her own life. Online, queer Egyptians were mourning, finding each other. I was alone, relegated to a tiny acreage on the outskirts of Knoxville, with only the humid air and crickets to keep me company. Nowhere to hide from myself.

I had come to the farm to write about my Coptic identity. My father was an Egyptian immigrant, my mother, a white Evangelical American. I had spent my life trying to reconcile what it meant to be Egyptian, to be Arab, to be white—to be both and neither, always slipping between.

My father was born in Sohag and fled Egypt as an adult, hours before the Six-Day War. He carried exile in his body, and in some ways, I did, too. I'd inherited my aunties' crescent-shaped eyes, my father's high, round cheeks. And yet, my American body—nose ring, tattoos, the way my hands reached instinctively for the curve of a woman's hip—marked me as something *other*. A shape I feared my family in Cairo, DC, and San Francisco would never embrace. I couldn't yet articulate it, so I looked outward.

I packed a suitcase full of other people's words—Arab journalists and poets, mixed-race essayists, even a legal dissertation on whether Copts were white. I searched for myself in their pages, desperate for someone to name the embodied experience I'd spent my life struggling to explain.

Yet somehow, between packing and lugging thirty-five pounds of books from New York to Appalachia, I had forgotten a hairbrush.

Day after day, as I sat on the porch, writing and rewriting sentences, my fine curls coiled tighter in the damp air. My skin deepened to a crisp olive. And while I struggled intellectually, my body remembered. It darkened as it does every summer, as effortlessly and predictably as the shifting light. All of me, unfurling into the wildness I had spent years trying—and failing—to smooth into submission.

As I wrote—about the inherent violence of whiteness, my queerness, the racism in my own home—I worried about the family in Egypt. At the same time, I was confronting the reality that, for those of us privileged enough to live in our own homes and in relative safety, remaining silent in the face of harm is its own form of complicity. And, as Audre Lorde reminds us, "Your silence will not protect you."

Silence has long been the currency of survival for Copts—particularly for women. We are taught that endurance is holy, that suffering is a virtue. That to speak too loudly is to unravel the very fabric of belonging.

Carolyn Ramzy's *Taslīm: We Are the Prophets* refuses silence. Like Lorde, she lives as an act of resistance. Following in Lorde's tradition, her work is both a model of autoethnographic refusal and a blueprint for cultural transformation. By claiming what others have tried to strip from her—her Copticity—while reckoning with its fractures and dissonance, she forges a path toward repair. More than just personal testimony; it is an invitation.

"I have often been accused of holding a grudge," Carolyn

cautions in the book's opening, almost as a warning. But from the very first pages, it is clear that she stands in a lineage of writers of colour who critique their communities not to abandon them, but because they know we can—and must—demand better. As James Baldwin writes of his great love of America, "[it is] exactly for this reason, I insist on the right to criticize her perpetually." Carolyn, too, insists on love through accountability. If her truth-telling creates rupture, it is rupture in service of a more expansive Coptic identity.

We Copts are many things—but we most certainly are not small. Nor is Carolyn's voice. She writes with the fullness of faith, desire, rage, and sex, refusing to shrink her literal and figurative body of work into a narrow inheritance. In *Coptic Porn Star*, she reclaims her sex as a sacred source of power, pomegranate jewels, a temptress with stones caught between her teeth, and without apology—

bringing the monks
down to their knees
to confess
to me.

In this world, it is not the woman who must be cleansed of her desire, but the monks and Orthobros who must reckon and forgive their own. Not to fear, repress, or project it onto us, but embrace it as whole. As Black voting rights activist Fannie Lou Hamer so famously said—"Nobody's free until everybody's free."

What if, Carolyn asks, faith was not about suffering, but joy?

Carolyn offers us glimpses: in the pleasure of kneading her tayta's *kaḥk* with her sons, in the liturgy lilting up through the floorboards, in the transgressive delight of a finger slipped into her mouth. In these pages, faith is not about endurance, but abundance. Our practice is "to imagine a life so possibly generous and abundant that we—and our children—can bravely say yes to living, and to do so resoundingly."

This is the work ahead of us. The movement from survival to joy, from inherited silence and shame to a faith that holds all of us—the women, queers, un/Orthodox, the exiled, and returning—unashamed and free. Shame isolates us. Healing happens in community.

We may leave the Church, or perhaps, like me, never fully had it to begin with—but it never fully leaves us. With those remains, we find our kin and build something new. "We are the prophets our mothers were looking for," Carolyn insists. If that is true—and I believe it is—we do more than inherit; we create. We build, together.

That summer on the farm, I thought I was writing in isolation. I was wrong. The next village is already forming—online, in basement services, in these pages. Listen closely. You'll find it in the slope of our hips, in my mixed hair—unwieldy, rising like a hymn.

Take, eat, drink. This work is a joyous labour. It belongs to us all.

Aly Tadros
New York City
February 2025

Glossary

One of the largest religious minorities in the Middle East, Coptic Christians nearly lost their first language, Coptic, by the twelfth century following the Arab conquest, which started as early as the seventh century. This gradual loss took close to seven hundred years and Coptic was largely relegated to liturgical worship and religious uses. Only a handful of families continue to speak the Coptic language today.

But as colonized and indigenous populations often do, we left our mark everywhere, and most of all, in the Egyptian Arabic vernacular. Unlike modern standard Arabic, Egypt's dialect is riddled with Coptic words, along with Ottoman, English, French and other assimilations. In short, you can hear our colonial history coming straight out of our mouths every time we speak, and most especially when we speak in English.

Here, I offer a glossary of some of the words I inherited in my Egyptian Arabic and that appear throughout this book. I use these words like a diaspora kid, calling on Arabic and Coptic fragmentations to bind the gaps in English, and to describe that wordless feeling of belonging to multiple somewheres and to nowhere, all at the same time.

abuna: Literally "our father," it is the honorary title of a Coptic Orthodox priest.

'ayb: Meaning "shame," *'ayb* is one of the most ubiquitous guiding words of Egyptian and Coptic girlhood. It is also one that never quite loses its grip, even as Coptic girls arrive into adulthood. Rather, notions of shame often discipline women's comportment, dress, and presence in public and private spaces. For Coptic women, *'ayb* also frames a notion of "sonic modesty," with the belief that women's voices have transgressive potentials to corrupt community morals. In turn, women often practice a form of "sonic veiling"—congregational blending—to ensure that their voices are not heard in overtly solo, loud, singular, or in non-congregational forms and may breach into *'ayb* territory during official ritual contexts.

'awra: The word *'ayb* also mirrors the widely understood notion of *'awra* to describe women's voices in sacral contexts. Unlike men's voices, women's voices are understood to carry sexual connotations—*'awra* literally means women's pudenda or privates— and are believed to have the potential to corrupt public morals. Egyptian clerics, including the previous Coptic Patriarch, Pope Shenouda III, often referred to Coptic women's solo voices during prayer as being naked or exposed.

'ayish shamsī: "Sun bread." This crusty sourdough bread is named for how it rises: often on rooftops and under the heat of the Upper Egyptian sun.

alḥan (s. laḥn): Coptic liturgical hymns. These hymns are venerated as the last remaining link to an ancient Egyptian ancestry, and form the bulk of the Coptic Orthodox canon. As Coptic music culture is gendered, only male readers, cantors, deacons, priests, bishops, and the Coptic patriarch can perform these hymns in any official capacity during liturgical worship. Women participate in congregational singing, and never in any official capacity during performances of prayers and traditional rites.

autoethnography: Tony Adams and Andrew Herrmann (2020) define autoethnography as a qualitative research method that uses personal experiences ("auto") to describe, interpret, and represent ("graphy") the beliefs, practices, and identities of a group or culture ("ethno"). This method is often found in the social sciences, including the disciplines of ethnomusicology and anthropology.

fūl: *Fūl* is a fava bean dish that is a staple of Egyptian cuisine. It is often prepared with olive oil or ghee, tahini, lemon, garlic, and cumin, and eaten with fresh pita or sun bread.

haram: "forbidden,"; often *haram* is twinned in a tight binary with the term *halal*, or "permissible." *Haram* is a familiar word that often shapes Coptic girlhood, namely what actions, sounds, foods, or clothing are considered allowed, honorable, and permissible for Coptic women and girls. The term *haram* often accompanies terms like *'ayb* and *'awra*, whose meaning extends notions of shame directly with women's pudenda or privates as flawed or disgraceful, and with the potential to upend community morals, decency, and even salvation.

kaḥk: Traditional cookies that often accompany wedding or religious celebrations (*eid*) such as the end of Ramadan, Easter, and Christmas. Given the laborious preparation of filling the buttery cookies with nuts, crimping the top, and dusting their faces with sugar, *kaḥk* baking is a social activity that regularly brings women together to chat and sing as they work.

al-kanīsa: The Egyptian colloquial Arabic term for church. Coptic hymnody, theology, and folk culture genders and sings about the Coptic Orthodox Church as a woman. Song tropes are replete with images that frame the Church as the "Bride of the Redeemer," "the Mother of the Martyrs," and a heavenly refuge from the hostilities of the world. Given that heaven and a Coptic afterlife are also gendered female (see *al-sama* below), women are often implicitly and explicitly taught to ascribe to qualities of selflessness, purity, and sacrifice that are ubiquitous in Coptic devotional songs (see *taratīl* and *taranīm* below) and Orthodox liturgical hymns (see *alḥan*).

kapt: Egyptian colloquial for "repression," the term also indexes a quiet understanding of sexual repression that is part and parcel of an Orthodox purity culture.

mulukhiya: This green herb soup (*tossa jute, Corchorus olitorius*) is often considered one of the national dishes of Egypt and has a distinct viscous texture that is brought to life with a *tasha* or splash of ghee, coriander, and garlic. Its smell and sound of the sizzling *tasha* is a hallmark of family kitchens, gatherings, and feasts, and is usually served with sun bread (*'ayish shamsī*), rice, and a favourite meat—or in some fasting seasons for Copts, with shrimp. Folklore has it that if you gasp as you mix the *tasha* with the *mulukhiya*, the sound wards off spirits hoping to spoil the dish by separating the stock from the viscous tossa jute.

Sa'īdī: Upper Egyptian; as the Nile flows downwards from the raised plains of southern Egypt to the lower passages of the delta, southern Egyptians are known as Upper Egyptians.

al-sama: heaven; gendered in Arabic as feminine, *al-sama* refers to an eternal and heavenly afterlife that is spent in an eternal act of *tasbīḥ* or sung praise. (See Ramzy 2014; Heo 2018).

samna: ghee made out of cow or buffalo milk and fat.

tasbīḥ: a heavenly state of eternal praise in the divine spirit of God, reconceiving traditional notions of heaven not as a place, but rather, as a sound. For Orthodox Copts, there is a firm comfort in knowing that the afterlife is bustling with sacred praise and community with the holy saints, both as ancestors and as kin, alongside earthly family, who have already proceeded to heaven. On earth, *tasbīḥ* or sung praise, consumes Coptic life as Copts sing to secure their place in eternity, and in the meantime, also recapitulate a heaven on this earth.

liturgy: The Orthodox liturgy. The height of Orthodox rituals happens when parishioners consume the Body (made of bread known as *orbana*) and Blood (*dam* or wine) of Christ in the most venerated and intimate act of Communion. In turn, the Eucharist or *al-tanāwil* binds Copts to one another, to their community, and to a sense of a heavenly belonging that is central to what the previous Coptic patriarch, Pope Shenouda III, called a "heavenly citizenship" to a "heavenly nation."

tayta: grandmother.

taratīl (s. tartīla): also known as *taranīm* and *tarnīma,* these paraliturgical songs have their roots in colonial missionary songs. Rather than translate them whole, Copts have assimilated and recalibrated these spiritual songs to contain their own Egyptian and Coptic folk melodies, Arabic colloquialisms, and for the most part, their Orthodox theology.

Works Cited

Absolon, Kathleen E. *Kaandossiwin: How We Come to Know, Indigenous Re-Search Methodologies*. Second edition. Halifax; Fernwood Publishing, 2022.

Adams, Tony and Andrew Herrmann. (2020) "Expanding our Autoethnographic Future" Journal of Autoethnography. 1 (1), 1–8.

Adams, Tony E., Stacy Linn Holman Jones, and Carolyn Ellis, eds. *Handbook of Autoethnography*. Second edition. New York, NY: Routledge, 2022.

Armanios, Febe. "Baking For God, the Virgin, and the Angels: Gendered Food Traditions in the Coptic Orthodox Community." *Making Minorities in the Middle East and North Africa,* Publisher, forthcoming.

Armanios, Febe. "Emerging Christian Media in Egypt: Clerical Authority and the Visualization of Women in Coptic Video Films." *International Journal of Middle East Studies,* Vol.45 (2013), 513-533.

Armanios, Febe. *Coptic Christianity in Ottoman Egypt*. Oxford University Press, 2011.

Armanios, Febe. "'The Virtuous Woman': Images of Gender in Modern Coptic Society." *Middle Eastern Studies,* Vol. 38, No. 1 (Jan., 2002), 110–130.

Ayad, Mariam F., editor. *Studies in Coptic Culture: Transmission and Interaction*. American University In Cairo Press, 2016.

Ayad, Mariam F., and Coptic Orthodox Church Centre (Stevenage, England). *Coptic Culture: Past, Present and Future*. The Coptic Orthodox Church Centre; David Brown Book Co., 2012.

Badran, Margot. *Feminists, Islam, and Nation Gender and the Making of Modern Egypt*. Course Book, Princeton University Press, 1995.

Bahgat, Peter. "A'arous El Fady El Kebteya | أعَروسَ الفادِى القِبطِية." (O Bride of the Reeder) *YouTube,* 10 Sept. 2020, www.youtube.com/watch?v=WV52mXzx8ck.

Baron, Beth. *Egypt as a Woman Nationalism, Gender, and Politics*. University of California Press, 2005, https://doi.org/10.1525/9780520940819.

Basilios, Archbishop. "Eucharistic Bread." The Coptic Encyclopedia, vol. 3, MacMillan, 1991, https://ccdl.claremont.edu/digital/collection/cce/id/808/rec/2.

Bochner, Arthur. *Evocative Autoethnography: Writing Lives and Telling Stories*. 1st ed. United Kingdom: Routledge, 2016.

Brown, Adrienne M. *Pleasure Activism: The Politics of Feeling Good*. Chico, CA: AK Press, 2019.

Britannica, The Editors of Encyclopaedia. "tossa jute". *Encyclopedia Britannica,* 12 Apr. 2018, https://www.britannica.com/plant/tossa-jute.

Coptic Church, et al. *The Three Liturgies of the Coptic Orthodox Church according to St. Basil, St. Gregory & St. Cyril*. St. Mark and St. Bishoy Coptic Orthodox Church, 1987.

Chandrashekar, Santosh. 2018. "Not a Metaphor: Immigrant of Color Autoethnography as a Decolonial Move." Cultural Studies, Critical Methodologies. 18(1): 72-79.

Doorn-Harder, Nelly van. *Contemporary Coptic Nuns*. University of South Carolina Press, 1995.

Farag, Lois M., editor. *The Coptic Christian Heritage: History, Faith, and Culture*. Routledge, 2014.

Faulkner, Sandra L. "Poetry Is Politics: An Autoethnographic Poetry Manifesto." *International Review of Qualitative Research,* vol. 10, no. 1, 2017, pp. 89–96.

Ghabrial, Sarah. "Gender, Power, and Agency in the Historical Study of the Middle East and North Africa." *International Journal of Middle East Studies* 48, no. 3 (2016): 561–64.

Gillespie, John. *The Egyptian Copts and Their Music*. [Institute of Coptic Studies, Dept. of Coptic Music], 1971.

Hanna, Trevena. "The Power of Coptic Women Saints: Historical and Analytical Study of Coptic Women Saints as Spiritual Models for Coptic Women in the Usa and Egypt." ProQuest Dissertations & Theses, 2020.

Hassan, Sana. *Christians versus Muslims in Modern Egypt: The Century-Long Struggle for Coptic Equality*. Oxford University Press, 2003.

Heo, Angie. *The Political Lives of Saints: Christian-Muslim Mediation in Egypt*. University of California Press, 2018.

Ibrahim, Samantha. "The Coptic #MeToo Era Has Finally Dawned. Here's Why You Should Care." *Medium* Magazine, 2 August 2020, https://medium.com/@egsrox95/the-coptic-metoo-era-has-finally-dawned-8b38a452c37e, accessed 10 October 2024.

Ibrahim, Mina. *Identity, Marginalisation, Activism, and Victimhood in Egypt: Misfits in the Coptic Christian Community*. London, UK: Palgrave MacMillian, 2022.

Kattan, Fadi, Nevine Abraham, Ryoko Sekiguchi, and Boutheina Bensalem. "An Oral History of Mouloukhiya from Egypt, Palestine, and Tunisia, and Japan." *The Markaz Review; Literature and Arts from the Center of the World,* January 24, 2022: https://themarkaz.org/an-oral-history-of-mouloukhiya-from-egypt-palestine-tunisia-and-japan/.

Lorde, Audre. *Uses of the Erotic: The Erotic as Power*. Out & Out Books, 1978.

Markos, Carol Nazmy. *Children of Day: Diasporic Ambivalence and Religious Revival among Coptic Orthodox Youth in Mississauga, Ontario*. Carleton University, 2024.

Mesat. "سؤال للبابا شنوده :ما رأي قداستكم في آنسة تقف على العشية وتردد التسبحة مع الشمامسة ؟ مي سات." [MeSat: "A Question for Pope Shenouda: What is Your Holiness' Opinion about a Woman who Stands to Sing from the Podium with the Deacons During Vesper Services?" YouTube, 9 Dec. 2018, www.youtube.com/watch?v=Jz4C5cdMCls.Shenouda III, Pope. *The Ordination of Women and Homosexuality : Two Lectures by Pope Shenouda III*. 1st ed, Coptic Orthodox Publishers Assoc., 1993.

Simpson, Leanne Betasamosake. "Constellations of Coresistance," in *As We Have Always Done: Indigenous Freedom Through Radical Resistance*. (Indigenous Americas. Minneapolis: Univ Of Minnesota Press, 2017): 211–232.

Philips, Miray. "'We Love Martyrdom, but We Also Love Life': Coptic Cultural Trauma between Martyrdom and Rights." *American Journal of Cultural Sociology* 11, no. 2 (2023): 220–47.

Ramzy, Carolyn. "Spiritual Transfiguration and 'Odit al-khawaga': Unpacking Race, Gender, and Coloniality in a Coptic Diaspora." *Jadaliyya,* 14 August 2023, https://www.jadaliyya.com/Details/45242.

Ramzy, Carolyn. "Coptic Women Sing Too," A Curated Multimedia Exhibit, American Religious Sound Projects, The Ohio State University and Michigan State University, 2022, https://gallery.religioussounds.osu.edu/copticwomensingtoo-exhibit-home/

Ramzy, Carolyn M. "Singing Heaven on Earth: Coptic Counter publics and Popular Song at Egyptian Mūlid Festivals." *International Journal of Middle East Studies* 49, no. 3 (2017): 375–94.

Ramzy, Carolyn. "Autotuned Belonging: Coptic Popular Song and the Politics of Neo-Pentecostal Pedagogies." *Ethnomusicology* 60, no. 3 (2016): 434–58.

Ramzy, Carolyn M. "To Die Is Gain: Singing a Heavenly Citizenship among Egypt's Coptic Christians." *Ethnos,* vol. 80, no. 5, 2015, pp. 649–70.

Rosald, Renato. *The Day of Shelly's Death: The Poetry and Ethnography of Grief*. Duke University Press, 2014.

Taranīm wa Madā'ḥ Muntakhaba. Cairo: Maktabat Al-Maḥabba Al-Qibtīyya (The Coptic Library of Love), 1986.

Tuck, Eve. "Suspending Damage: A Letter to Communities." *Harvard Educational Review* 79, no. 3 (2009): 409–28.

Tuck Eve and K Wayne Yang. 2012. "Decolonization is not a Metaphor." *Decolonization: Indigeneity, Education & Society*. 1(1): 1–40.

Youssef, Joseph. *Becoming Saints: Coptic Orthodox Monasticism, Exemplarity, Negotiating Christian Virtue*. University of Toronto, 2019.

Youssef, Mariam. *Gendered Paradigms in Theologies of Survival: Silenced to Survive*. Lexington Books, 2020.

Youssef, Mariam. *Going Home: Exploring Death and Gender in Diasporic Coptic Community*. Lexington Books, forthcoming.

Zacharia, Marcus. "Tackling Sex Education and Sexual Abuse in the Egyptian-Canadian Diaspora" *Egyptian Streets,* 4 April 2021, https://egyptianstreets.com/2021/04/04/tackling-sex-education-and-sexual-abuse-in-the-egyptian-canadian-diaspora/.